The Third House:
Lobbyists, Money, and Power in Sacramento

The Third House:
Lobbyists, Money, and Power in Sacramento

Jay Michael and Dan Walters
with Dan Weintraub

Berkeley Public Policy Press
Institute of Governmental Studies
University of California, Berkeley
2002

Library of Congress Cataloging-in-Publication Data

Michael, Jay.
    The third house : lobbyists, money, and power in Sacramento / Jay Michael and
Dan Walters ; with Dan Weintraub.
      p. cm.
    ISBN 0-87772-397-4
    1. Lobbyists--California. 2. Lobbying--California. I. Walters, Dan. II. Weintraub,
Dan. III. Title.

    JK8774.5 .M53 2001
    328.794'078--dc21   2001037559

Contents

Preface

It's been said that in all respects except the technical fact that it is a state, California more accurately resembles a separate nation. Indeed, given its huge population, its breathtaking diversity, its historic independence, and its immensely powerful economy, it is the equivalent of a major European nation. Not surprisingly, there's a substantial body of scholarship and literature about the California Legislature that acknowledges the state's powerful place in national and even international affairs.

These publications include dry statistical studies, the musings of political scientists and historians and, most interestingly, insider accounts written by the odd legislator who's capable of writing a simple declarative sentence without a ghost at the keyboard. But no matter what the origin or form, they tend to focus on what politicians do, largely omitting the central role that the Capitol's 1,000-plus lobbyists play in shaping the policies that affect Californians. This book is an effort to fill the void, based on the experiences and observations of the authors, one a retired lobbyist and the other a working journalist, who collectively have well over a half-century of daily contact with what happens in the Capitol.

We hope to give readers a working knowledge of the policymaking process as it really functions, as opposed to the sanitized version one finds in civics textbooks, so they will be able to view daily accounts of Capitol events in a new and more sophisticated light. Our most consistent theme is that money is the Capitol's preoccupation, both the money to be gained or lost by interest groups in pursuing their various goals inside the building, and the money that those groups "donate" to politicians to secure access and favorable votes.

The seventh and final chapter by Dan Weintraub is adapted from a series of articles he wrote for *The Orange County Register* in 2000. We include it because it is an exquisitely detailed account of one lobbyist's year-long effort to enact one bill and underscores the inescapable conclusion that when moneyed interests clash with "public interest" advocates, the former almost always have their way. Public interest lobbyists just don't have all the tools—which we describe as a "three-legged stool"—that are vital to success in the California Capitol.

Jay Michael and Dan Walters
Sacramento, 2001

Foreword

The origins of this book go back many years. Jay Michael left city management in 1966 to become the Sacramento representative for the University of California, and journalist Dan Walters began to cover the Capitol in 1975.

Michael arrived on the Sacramento scene just in time to see his new boss Clark Kerr fired, but stayed on to serve under Charles Hitch, whose tenure coincided with the administration of Governor Ronald Reagan. Michael left the University to serve as the chief lobbyist for the high-powered California Medical Association and—until his recent retirement—related health policy organizations.

Dan Walters' Sacramento career has spanned the administrations of Governors Jerry Brown, George Deukmejian, Pete Wilson and now Gray Davis. From the Oregon line to the Mexican border, Walters has explored the forces underlying the making of California public policy. Critical, but objective, his columns constitute must reading for serious students of the state's political scene.

Together, there could be no better guides than Michael and Walters to California's "third house," the lobbyists who represent the several hundred interest groups shaping public policy in this, the nation's largest state and the world's fifth largest economy. These legislative advocates—ranging from volunteers to highly paid professionals—are at the heart of the policy process. Unrestricted by term limits, they are often the most knowledgeable individuals concerning the impact of the complex and controversial details that are the foundation of the laws and regulations (and court decisions) that affect the lives of Californians in so many ways.

In 1949, the distinguished writer Carey McWilliams described the Sacramento scene as a "marketplace," where interests not people are represented and bid for allotments of state power. Fifty years later, we know all too little about the inner workings of this "marketplace." Professor Rogan Kersh at Syracuse's Maxwell School writes, focusing on the Congress: "The influence of organized interest groups in America's pluralist political system is well chronicled by scholars. Yet interest-group lobbyists have been studied remarkably little in practice." This is no less the case for California. Studies abound on governors, the legislature, elections, political parties. But the "third house" is little examined and even less understood.

Michael and Walters address this imbalance. They draw back the curtain on the changing patterns of legislative advocacy in Sacramento—Samish and Unruh, term limits and elections, horse racing and Indian casinos, insurance and health care, changing demographics and the initiative are among the many issues and personalities that color the pages that follow. Readers will emerge with new insights into the Capitol scene and thank Jay Michael and Dan Walters for sharing their knowledge, drawn from a combined experience of more than 60 years. We are in their debt.

Eugene C. Lee
Professor Emeritus of Political Science
Director, Institute of Governmental Studies, 1967–88

CHAPTER 1

Who Are These People Called Lobbyists?

"A party machine can be challenged at the polls, but as long as Artie controls the interest groups his power is beyond dispute."—Carey McWilliams on pioneer lobbyist Artie Samish

It's late August and even at 10 p.m., the temperature in downtown Sacramento is stuck in the high 80s as summer heat radiates from concrete sidewalks and the marble walls of high-rise office buildings. The powerful air conditioners atop California's wedding cake Capitol building are humming and maintaining what its thermostats say is a comfortable 72 degrees in its wide corridors. But in one of those corridors, which run along the rear of the chambers of both legislative houses, dozens of well-dressed men and women try not to sweat as they stand shoulder-to-shoulder. They're chatting among themselves, whispering into pocket phones, glancing at television monitors mounted near the corridor ceiling, munching on stale doughnuts, trying to work their way toward doorways guarded by legislative sergeants-at-arms and, most of all, worrying about what legislators on the other side of the wall are doing. A few lobbyists escape from the pack and amuse themselves by leaning over the railing of the Capitol's rotunda and pitching coins into the crown of a statue of Queen Isabella on the floor below. Few, if any, of the coins actually make it into the crown and on mornings after a long session, the floor is littered with misdirected coins. Some of the lobbyists slip across the street to a bar where television monitors tuned to the legislative floors allow lobbyists to monitor the action while fortifying themselves for battles yet to come. The less alcohol-inclined repair to the Capitol's

6th floor cafeteria, which remains open late and keeps its TV sets tuned to the floors.

It's the last night of the annual legislative session, and lawmakers of the nation's richest and most populous state are churning their way through hundreds of bills, some of which are undergoing last-second amendments to change their effect, as the midnight adjournment nears. What the legislators do, or don't do, in the next 120 minutes could mean hundreds of millions, even billions, of dollars to businesses, labor unions, professional organizations, and government agencies. And these groups depend on their lobbyists—what Capitol insiders have long called "the third house"—to protect their interests.

They've spent months, even years, gathering information, attending legislative hearings, negotiating with each other, with legislators and/or with legislative staff members, schmoozing at restaurants and on fishing trips and golf excursions, spending thousands of their clients' dollars on tickets to campaign fundraising events, flacking the media, and organizing outside-the-Capitol influence. It is all aimed at strengthening the "three-legged stool" of effective political action. Money, grassroots action, and lobbying expertise, veterans of the trade believe, interact with one another to create a synergy that's essential to success in policy arenas. They know that the public face of politics—the campaigns that pander to various constituencies, the legislative hearings, the debates on bills, the news conferences and media events—are just for show, and that lobbyists represent the real focus of the Capitol that most of the public doesn't even know exists.

As midnight approaches, some issues have been settled and some lobbyists have the luxury of skipping the last, frantic hours of the legislative session, their efforts done for the year—if they can bear to stay away from the action. But for hundreds of lobbyists, this is the moment of truth, when they learn whether their work will pay off. After the final vote is taken, the gavel bangs for the last time and legislators scatter, lobbyists will tote up their wins and losses and devote the autumn to convincing their employers that what's been done has been worth the effort, a task many consider to be more difficult than lobbying itself, and persuading them to replenish, and perhaps expand, their lobbying budgets for another year of political combat. Chances are, when legislators return to Sacramento a few months later to begin the process again, they will be greeted by even more lobbyists representing even more clients.

Who are these people? Why do they command fees that top-drawer lawyers might envy? How much influence do they wield in a forum that's supposed to conduct the public's business? Does that influence, whatever it may be, ultimately undermine the public interest, or is it vital to effective lawmaking? There are no single answers to any of these questions because they are utterly dependent on widely varying viewpoints. Politicians, clients, political reformers, the media, voters, and lobbyists themselves have highly divergent definitions of lobbyists and their role in political decision making, to wit:

- Politicians, especially those in office, see lobbyists as conduits for campaign funds, as connectors to interest group and individual constituencies that can be important sources of political support, as sources of legislative ideas that will enhance their political careers, as sounding boards for assessing the impact of political actions, as sources of information, and as protectors when the politicians' actions alienate other interests. While there may be personal and social ties between politicians and lobbyists, there is also an inherent level of mistrust in their relationships, since each group is looking to the other for some benefit. And politicians often envy the high incomes of lobbyists—which may explain why so many former officeholders go into the trade themselves.

- Clients see lobbyists as professional advocates who use their knowledge, connections, and other assets to reduce regulatory and tax burdens, gain advantages over competitors, block competitors from getting an edge on them, gain budget appropriations, or resolve conflicts in the client's favor.

- Political reform groups are certain that lobbyists corrupt a political system that would otherwise be free of special interest influence—or at least they paint such a picture to maintain the faith of their members. As reformers such as Common Cause portray the system, lobbyists buy access through their clients' campaign money, get legislators elected to do their bidding, disenfranchise the public, and contribute to the popular malaise about politics. They are willing to suspend or severely limit constitutional guarantees of free speech, private association, and petitioning government to root out what they regard as evil, by imposing tight restrictions on campaign contributions and even lobbyists' conversations with politicians.

- The media have a bifurcated view of and relationship with the Capitol lobbying corps. While news accounts—and even more often, newspaper editorials—often reflect the political reformers' dark view of lobbying, political reporters themselves often depend on lobbyists as sources of reliable and timely information, much as politicians do. Lobbyists also become involved in the never-ending cat-and-mouse game between politicians and the media. Politicians, of course, are constantly seeking more favorable images for themselves in the media, which are the primary vehicle by which voters form their opinions of politicians. Politicians often believe that reporters are out to make them look bad, while journalists believe that politicians are not trustworthy sources of information because they skew the facts to make themselves look good. Still, among the various component groups of the Capitol, the press often sees lobbyists—their somewhat sinister public image notwithstanding—as neutral arbiters of what's accurate and what's not.

- Voters, and the broader public, often reflect the negative stereotypes of lobbyists flowing from reformers and the media. In part, this popular view of lobbyists and their activities reflects an ignorance that just about everyone directly or indirectly employs lobbyists through their taxes to local governments and schools, their labor unions and/or their trade associations. Even the very poor have lobbyists working on their behalf in Sacramento, as do the political reformers who publicly decry the influence of lobbyists even as they lobby themselves.

• Lobbyists see themselves as professional, disinterested gladiators in a dangerous arena, under tremendous pressure from their clients and employers to deliver, as strategists and tacticians whose advice is sought in clarifying and delivering political objectives, as experts in the art of persuasion, as coordinators of disparate resources—even as protectors of the public interest by their ability to spot and short-circuit ill-conceived legislative proposals.

All of these views are quite accurate, as far as they go. But one must incorporate all of them to get a full picture of why a lobbyist's skills are in demand and how they go about performing for their employers.

The term "lobbying" evolved from the early days of the American republic, when pleaders for various causes and interests would gather in the lobbies of Congress and state legislatures and buttonhole lawmakers. Until a few years ago, that practice had its counterpart in Sacramento as lobbyists congregated near the front entrance to the state Assembly chambers, even though the Senate relegated them to the back hallway. Former Assembly Speaker Willie Brown banished lobbyists to the rear after concluding that allowing them at the front door was giving the Assembly a bad image. It was during a period when lawmakers, legislative staffers and lobbyists were being prosecuted for offering or taking bribes and the Legislature's stature had fallen to an all-time low.

Whether welcomed at the front door or confined to the back hallway, however, lobbyists have become an integral piece of the legislative process in the Capitol and a growth industry. Today, at least 1,200 men and women—the ranks of the latter have swollen dramatically in recent years—earn tens of millions of dollars from thousands of clients to influence what the Legislature, the governor, and dozens of state agencies do, reflecting state government's exponentially expanding reach as the state itself has become more culturally and economically complex.

It's been estimated that the various decision-making arms of the state directly control at least $400 billion each year, equivalent to a third of the state's personal income and the economic output of a medium-sized nation, and have indirect power over countless tens of billions of dollars more, not to mention nonmonetary cultural issues. The rates that Californians pay for utilities, the premiums they pay for insurance, the quality of their schools and colleges, the size of their tax bills, the ability of local governments to supply police, fire, and library services, the congestion of highways, the cost of homes, health and safety conditions in the workplace, the legalization or prohibition of gambling, the marketing of alcoholic beverages, how many felons are locked up in prison, the availability and price of medical care—even which breed of horse can race at which track on which day—are decided by the governor, his appointees, legislators, or other elected state officials.

Thousands of specific interest groups are affected by those decisions, and they employ lobbyists, either directly on their payrolls or through contracts, to represent them in the halls of government, much as lawyers represent clients in the courtroom. But while courts operate by fairly strict, even arcane, procedural rules, the world of the lobbyist is much more complicated and much less formal. Carey McWilliams, the fabled analyst of California's post-World War II development, once described the Capitol this way: "Interests, not people, are represented in Sacramento . . . the marketplace of California where grape growers and sardine fishermen, morticians and osteopaths bid for allotments of state power." With a substitution of interests, the observation is as valid today as when it was first written more than a half-century earlier. It would be fair to say that 200 to 300 of the 1,200 registered lobbyists, the cream of the crop, routinely and reliably call the shots on at least 80 percent of the issues coming before the Legislature and play major roles in the outcome of decisions in other governmental or political forums, such as administrative agencies and the initiative process.

To fully appreciate the central, even commanding, role that lobbyists play in the Capitol of the 21st century, one must understand how California and its political decision-making process evolved in the 19th and 20th, and particularly how lobbyists shaped what happened from the earliest days of the state in the mid-19th century. When, for example, the first Legislature met in San Jose in 1849, those seeking positions in the brand-new state government developed the practice of setting up bars and dispensing free drinks to the legislators to win favors. As recounted by historians, a state senator named Thomas Green, who wanted to become commander of the state militia, would holler "a thousand drinks for everyone" at the end of every Senate session, finally pouring his way, as it were, into the generalship he craved and enshrining "The Legislature of a thousand drinks" in the pages of history. The Gold Rush brought tens of thousands of newcomers to the state, and they jousted constantly for land, water, navigation rights, and other exploitative advantages in the Legislature, which moved often before settling in Sacramento (by trickery, residents of the previous capital, Benicia, always contended) and building the Capitol that, having been restored in the 1970s, looks much as it did in 1900. Favor-seekers of the late 19th century routinely plied legislators with liquor, women, and cash, but as the century drew to an end, more respectable, if not more ethical, forces came to dominate the Capitol.

The dawn of the 20th century saw California, blessed with immense natural resources, beginning to show the economic promise that would become reality as it developed into the planet's fifth most powerful economy were it a separate nation. The Gold Rush that brought thousands of fortune-seekers to California a half-century earlier had faded, but the state's reputation as a place for new beginnings was still intact. While loggers chopped their way through the state's huge stands of timber, including the towering redwood trees of the North Coast, and corporate mining operations replaced the blue-jeaned gold-panners in exploiting the state's mineral wealth, railroads encouraged farmers to settle in the state's broad and fertile river valleys, especially the 450-mile-long Central Valley, to justify their investment in track and locomotives, while land speculators laid out entire new cities.

The railroads, especially the huge Southern Pacific, virtually owned the state through their ownership of vast tracts of land and their control of shipping and freight rates. Muckraker Frank Norris's novel "The Octopus," based on a bloody 1880 clash at Mussel Slough, southwest of Fresno, between farmers and railroad agents over the ownership of land, dramatized the turn-of-the-century conflicts that gave rise to reformers such as Hiram Johnson, who was born in Sacramento, saw first-hand how the Capitol had been corrupted and devoted his governorship to breaking the stranglehold of the railroads on California politics.

Southern Pacific had been fashioned by early California railroad tycoons from the Central Pacific, one of the two builders of the transcontinental railroad, and a host of smaller lines, extending the SP's tracks from one end of California to the other and its freight and passenger network through the Southwest from Arizona, New Mexico, and Texas to New Orleans. Its rapid expansion was fueled by the same monetary enticement that had made the cross-country line possible: huge tracts of free land on either side of the new lines as they were built. SP eventually acquired more than 11 million acres of land in California. It founded dozens of towns and lured farmers from Eastern states to buy its land, especially in the fertile Central Valley, and use the railroad for freight and passengers.

Southern Pacific's virtual monopoly on transportation in California during the late 19th century—there were few roads, almost no other railroads and SP also owned ferries and river steamers—gave it the opportunity to charge what many customers considered to be usurious rates for its services. Discontent among farmers led to political clashes—and a gun battle at Mussel Slough—and fueled demands for reform in how the railroad was regulated and taxed. But through its control of the state Legislature, SP was able to stave off demands for rate regulation. William Herrin, SP's chief counsel, became California's first powerful lobbyist, openly dispensing bribes to legislators in Sacramento—including free round-trip tickets on SP's passenger trains. Later, when anti-SP reforms were enacted, one of them was a prohibition on legislators' receiving freebies from transportation companies, and as late as the 1990s, some lawmakers ran afoul of the law by accepting gifts of airline tickets.

Hiram Johnson gained fame as a prosecutor of San Francisco's graft-ridden city government, and in 1910, the reformist Lincoln-Roosevelt League—an offshoot of the Republican party aligned with Theodore Roosevelt—ran Johnson as its candidate for governor. He was swept into office with a phalanx of reform-minded legislators, and the newcomers quickly enacted a flock of political and economic changes that continue to reverberate today. Viewing the railroad-influenced political parties as "vessels of corruption," Johnson and his allies championed reforms, such as direct primaries and cross-filing, that weakened parties and strengthened, or so they believed, individual voters. A Public Utilities Commission would oversee railroads and other monopolies, and the Legislature itself was to be kept in check through the initiative and referendum, which allowed voters to bypass the Capitol altogether to make law, or to overturn a law enacted by the Legislature and the governor. Johnson captured a U.S. Senate seat in 1916 and served nearly 30 years in the Senate, but the progressive-reformist tradition slumbered for a generation, until another former prosecutor, Earl Warren, woke it up in the 1940s.

The 1930s and 1940s saw California's economy undergo a major transformation, and with change came evolution in the nature of lobbying in Sacramento. The agrarian-resource economy that had been the basis for Southern Pacific's expansion gave way to manufacturing and to entirely new industries, such as motion pictures. The 1930s also saw a sharp expansion of state government, mirroring what was happening in New Deal Washington, and with that came renewed interest in influencing what the governor and the Legislature were doing. The time, in other words, was ripe for Artie Samish, who came to fill a vacuum that Hiram and the reformers had inadvertently created in their zealous campaign against political parties.

A one-time low-level clerk in San Francisco city government, Samish had come to Sacramento in 1918 to take an equally menial job in the Legislature, albeit one that gave him a detailed knowledge of legislative mechanics. In the early 1920s he switched to lobbying and after serving an apprenticeship to another lobbyist, set himself up as a "consultant" to trade associations, many of which he created and scored an early coup by gaining enactment of an amendment to the state public utilities code that gave a major competitive advantage to one of his first clients, a consortium of local bus lines on the San Francisco Peninsula that was later to become the nationwide Greyhound bus system. From that initial triumph, trade associations of liquor wholesalers, horse racing tracks, and other interests pumped huge fees into Samish's bank account in return for his uncanny ability to get friendly legislation passed.

Samish invented a system that was later put to productive use by other lobbyists and legislative leaders, one he called "select and elect." As Samish later explained in his book, *The Secret Boss of California,* a fascinating inside look at Sacramento in the 1930s, 1940s and 1950s: "First organize the interest group and convince the members to contribute funds for their own interests. Then, spend the money wisely to elect those who would be friendly to those interests." Continuing, Samish wrote, "I didn't care whether a man was a Republican or a Democrat or a Prohibitionist. I didn't care whether he voted against free love or for the boll weevil. All I cared about was how he voted on legislation affecting my clients." Thus, Samish was careful not to involve himself in the bigger issues of the day, as long as his clients' relatively minor interests were protected. Samish reinforced his position by maintaining a wide-open suite of rooms at the Senator Hotel, just across L Street from the Capitol, in which legislators could obtain food and drinks virtually around the clock, and by employing a coterie of spies who kept him constantly informed about anything he needed to know. He made certain that legislators in his flock could supplement their scanty legislative salaries with perfectly legal outside income, such as retainers for lawyers or policy sales for insurance brokers. Samish considered outright bribery to be not only illegal but "stupid, both on the part of the legislators and the lobbyists."

The system that Samish pioneered has not only survived but, in recent years, returned with a vengeance as legislative leadership has declined. The current term of art is "targeting," in which a legislative district is chosen by its demographic makeup or voting history as ripe for change, a candidate is selected for his or her friendliness to the intervening interest group's goals, and enough money is provided through various sources to help the selected politician win the election. When it's done skillfully and often enough, as Samish first discovered, the interest group achieves a Legislature so tilted in its favor that contests with rival interests are over before they begin.

What Samish's clients wanted, as often as not, was state regulation that would protect them against competitors and/or ensure their ability to set prices. Perhaps the most notorious examples of such interest-friendly regulation were the so-called "fair trade" liquor laws that allowed liquor manufacturers to set retail prices and, in effect, made price competition illegal—a pattern that continues in Sacramento. The most intense lobbying is conducted over issues of state regulation. Big business—automakers, computer companies or oil companies—is a relatively small player in the Capitol. The biggest employers of lobbyists are interest groups subject to state regulation, such as insurance companies, health care providers, gambling casinos, personal injury lawyers, and other governments. The governor and the Legislature set the rules by which they prosper or wither and that gives them a direct interest in affecting what's done in the Capitol.

One example regarding liquor laws illustrates the syndrome. While the Samish-spawned "fair trade" laws governing liquor sales were later wiped out by the courts, a few statutes remain unmolested, one of them being the "tied-house" law that prohibits anyone engaged in one level of the liquor industry—manufacturing, wholesaling, or retailing—from also engaging in another. The rationale for the law, however flawed, is that it prohibits monopolies. The practical effect is to require any company wishing to operate on more than one level to hire a lobbyist and come to the Legislature for a bill granting a special exemption. Thus, when the huge Seagram's liquor conglomerate bought a controlling interest in MCA, the parent corporation of Universal Studios, in the 1990s the deal was put on hold until the Legislature passed a tied-house exemption because Universal sells liquor at its theme parks. Or when wineries wanted to become retail sellers of wine or open liquor-dispensing restaurants, they had to get case-by-case exemptions. A blanket overhaul, and possibly repeal, of the tied-house laws might be warranted, but that would reduce the trade in exemptions, which would reduce lobbying income and the opportunities for legislators to expand their fundraising hit lists.

Samish wasn't shy about what he did. He referred to himself as "the guy who gets things done" and allowed himself to be quoted in newspapers and magazines about the power he wielded in Sacramento. "I am the governor of the Legislature," he once boasted. "To hell with the governor of California." But his boastfulness and hubris were his undoing after decades of running the show—a syndrome that was to afflict other lobbyists from time to time. Four decades after Samish's reign had ended, for example, one of the most powerful lobbyists of his era, insurance industry advocate Clay Jackson, was sent to federal prison after offering to bribe a legislator who had been publicly identified as a federal target himself. The politician was wearing a radio transmitter, and the tapes of their conversations, later played to a jury, were Jackson's undoing.

Samish's first flirtation with serious trouble came in the late 1930s when he and his liquor clients got into a squabble with a prohibitionist Republican governor, Frank Merriam, and the governor formed an alliance with a Democratic state senator from Los Angeles, Culbert Olson, who was later to become Merriam's successor in the governorship. Merriam and Olson sponsored an investigation of Samish by the Sacramento County district attorney's office, which hired private investigator Howard Philbrick. Investigators convened a grand jury, began taking testimony about Samish's activities, and subpoenaed the famous influence peddler and his records. Samish took it all jocularly, hamming it up for reporters and playing jokes on his pursuers, and was pleased when the grand jury didn't even mention him in its report. Philbrick, however, wrote a lengthy report—which Samish blocked from publication in the Legislature's official records. The report, printed and distributed by Governor Merriam, portrayed Samish as a sinister influence on the Capitol "but all his words didn't prove a goddamn thing," Samish later crowed. And Samish later claimed credit for helping Olson defeat Merriam in the 1938 governor's election.

A decade later, social commentator Carey McWilliams, in his landmark book *California: The Great Exception,* cited Samish's clash with Merriam as proof of the lobbyist's omnipotence in Sacramento and laid out how he was able to fill the vacuum that Johnson and the antiparty reformers had created. "What Mr. Samish has done . . . is to convert the interest-group into a political machine which functions independently of the party," McWilliams observed.

From the lobbyists' point of view, of course, this represents a distinct advance in the forms of political control. A party machine can be challenged at the polls but as long as Artie controls the interest groups his power is beyond dispute. Theoretically his power could be challenged by the interest groups he represents but—and this is the key to the structure of power he has fashioned—these groups enjoy, despite the costs, great advantages from his representation. In the first place, the state takes over the function and also the expense of policing the particular industry against "unfair trade practices"—an enormous saving in itself. In the second place, each industry group and each individual member of this group is spared the trouble and expense of dealing with individual politicians. Control must be centralized to be effective and, in California where there are no old-style party bosses and little party discipline, business and industry must have some "protection" against the endless demands of free-lance politicians. . . .

For in the absence of party machines, given the cross-filing system and the trade association machines which he controls, he can nominate and elect candidates in many districts by the expenditure of nominal sums. Furthermore, his power cannot be exposed since the most powerful economic interest-groups of the state are his clients. For example, he keeps up-to-the-minute files on the allocation of advertising by his various clients. If a newspaper is "unfriendly," advertising is promptly removed.

McWilliams' description of how Samish operated in the Capitol was quite accurate, as the lobbyist's own first-person account would later demonstrate. But McWilliams was wrong in believing that Samish was untouchable, as much as that appeared to be true in the later 1940s. Even as McWilliams' book was being published in 1949, Samish's downfall was taking shape—and it came in the person of journalist Lester Velie, a latter-day muckraker who wanted to do an article about Samish for *Collier's* magazine.

At first, as Samish later recounted it, he bragged about various exploits and dazzled Velie with his knowledge of who Velie had already interviewed for the article, thus proving how well-informed he was about Sacramento.

"I even told him about how my Gestapo worked," Samish recalled. "I had 25 people stationed around the Capitol, and they were truly undercover workers. Nobody knew they worked for me. In fact, they didn't even know each other."

Velie's article about Samish and his power paralleled much of what McWilliams had said in his book, albeit in more detail. But as Samish later lamented, "The trouble was, he couldn't tell when I was clowning." Samish's playful boasts made him seem even more powerful than he was. "But it wasn't anything I said that had the biggest reaction from the *Collier's* articles. It was the answer that Governor Earl Warren gave when he was asked who had more influence over the Legislature, the governor or Artie Samish." Warren told Velie that "on matters that affect his clients, Artie unquestionably has more power than the governor."

And then there was that picture that accompanied the *Collier's* piece, the one of Samish, wearing a straw boater and sitting on a chair holding a ventriloquist's dummy. "I not only supplied Mr. Velie with quotes; I gave him a prize picture as well," Samish said later. "When his photographer was taking some shots of me, I told him: 'You want the real picture? I'll give you something that tells the whole story.' Then I produced a little ventriloquist's dummy, a cheerful hobo with white gloves and a top hat. I planted the dummy in front of me and said, 'That's the way I lobby. That's my Legislature. That's Mr. Legislature. 'How are you today, Mr. Legislature?'"

Not surprisingly, the *Collier's* account of Samish's wheeler-dealer ways— and that photograph—stirred up a political storm. It was one thing to control the Legislature, or at least strongly influence it, and it was quite another to rub politicians' noses in their subservient status in a national magazine. Politicians and editorial writers demanded an investigation—as if they didn't know what Samish had been doing all those years. Samish himself seemed nonplussed, even amused, by the sudden cries of outrage.

"I got no apology for the articles," he told the San Francisco Press Club, "and I got no explanations. It would be easy for me to cop a plea and say that I had been misquoted. But hell, I wouldn't do that if any of you got me in hot water, and I certainly wouldn't do it to a fine reporter like Lester Velie. Ninety percent of what he wrote was true. The only trouble was that he had some preconceived notions of how California politics operate. And he used his information to try and substantiate those notions of his." Samish even more or less portrayed himself as a reformer, saying he would cooperate with an investigation of influence peddling, if all lobbyists and all interest groups were subjected to the same scrutiny. "If the result of the investigation is to eliminate all lobbyists— including myself—I'll be the most pleased man in the state, because I know that the people had won back their government."

A legislative investigation was mounted, replete with a special prosecutor who had participated in the Japanese war crimes trials a few years earlier, and Samish was the lead witness as hearings opened, as unapologetic and playful as ever. He even half-seriously offered to give up his special interest clients and become "the people's lobbyist." The investigation, however, focused almost solely on him and never delved into the activities of other lobbyists and interest groups and resulted in a legislative resolution condemning him, authored by a legislator Samish had helped elect. But Samish continued to do business as usual in the Senator Hotel, playing host to a steady stream of lawmakers from the across the street. And, ironically enough, the late 1940s and early 1950s, when Samish was enjoying the peak of his influence over legislation affecting his clients, considered by historians to be the golden age of California policymaking, when Governor Earl Warren and legislators built highways, colleges, and parks and created a legacy of high-quality government services that never was to be surpassed, or even equaled. As obsequious as they may have been to Samish and other lobbyists on their peculiar interests, legislators of the era took a broad and high-minded attitude on matters of overarching public interest, on which there was little or no overt lobbying. It was if there were two Capitols, one dealing with the big issues of a fast-growing and fast-changing California and another with the minute, if lucrative, matters affecting the employers of Samish and other lobbyists. The two faces of the Capitol were rarely in conflict with one another, and Samish took pride in the progressive policies implemented by those he helped elect.

The most concrete reform to evolve from the *Collier's* article was legislation initially sponsored by Warren—pieces of which are still in effect—that would require lobbyists and their clients to register and report their financial dealings, prohibit legislators and other public employees from lobbying, and prohibit lobbyists from basing their fees on their success in getting legislation passed or defeated. Nearly 50 years later, a lobbyist for the State Bar ran afoul of the latter provision when it was revealed that he had a contract with a bonus if he succeeded in getting the Legislature to raise the dues that lawyers were compelled to pay to the State Bar. Samish himself was scornful of the lobbyist regulations. "How did it affect me?" he later wrote.

> Not at all. Oh, perhaps I had to change some of my procedures. But I went on doing business at the same old stand, watching after the interests of my clients. . . . The whole point had been missed by everyone concerned. All the rules and regulations in the world wouldn't change the influence of lobbyists like myself in Sacramento. . . . As long as the people of California paid only $1,200 a year to the men who made their laws, as long as most candidates were elected in the primaries, as long as most citizens didn't even know the names of their senators and assemblymen, then the people would not get rid of Art Samish.

If the initial reaction to the *Collier's* article didn't faze Samish, the national attention it focused on Sacramento led to his downfall as Tennessee Senator Estes Kefauver made California—San Francisco specifically—a stop on his national tour of hearings dealing with organized crime and called Samish to testify about his dealings with clients, especially those in the liquor industry, and how he distributed money to get friendly candidates elected to the Legislature. A Kefauver committee report focused on Samish's cash dealings and recommended an investigation by the Justice Department and the Internal Revenue Service. Samish may have been able to laugh his way through state legislative hearings but getting the feds on his tail was another matter. IRS agents spent more than two years poring over his spotty financial records, and the Justice Department's criminal division, headed by an Earl Warren protégé with whom Samish had clashed years earlier, pushed the investigation. In 1953, Samish was indicted for evading taxes on a series of checks that he had received from a liquor industry client. He was convicted on eight counts after a trial he said he didn't take seriously, culminating in a three-year term in federal prison. His defense, fines, back taxes, and restitution cost Samish more than a million dollars—as well as his lobbying practice.

As the three-decade-long Samish era of Capitol politics came to a close in the mid-1950s, another episode was beginning, one dominated by an equally rotund, equally fun-loving, and equally bright politician from southern California. Jesse Marvin Unruh took control of the "select and elect" system that Samish had created and shifted it into the Legislature itself, changing the culture of the Capitol and altering the dynamics of lobbying in the process.

Jesse Unruh was emblematic of two of California's most powerful social forces in the mid-20th century: the migration to California from Texas, Arkansas, Oklahoma, and other "Dust Bowl" states, and the impact of returning World War II veterans on California's economy, social structure, and politics. The son of a Texas sharecropper, Unruh—particularly if he had had a drink or two—would vividly describe going to school barefooted, even in the winter and other aspects of a "dirt poor" upbringing. "How poor were we?" a colleague once quoted him as saying. "We were so poor I didn't known that other people took baths on Saturday night until I was ten. After I found out, I took one every Saturday night in a horse trough, if the weather wasn't too bad." As a teenager when World War II broke out, Unruh hitchhiked to California to get a job in a defense plant, sleeping in a chicken coop at his brother's house in Hawthorne, then returning to the Midwest and knocking around until he found a navy recruiter who would overlook his flat feet after the attack on Pearl Harbor. After spending the war in the remote Aleutian Islands, Unruh returned to California and used the GI Bill to get a degree in economics from the University of Southern California, becoming active in student politics and honing his commitment to populist liberalism with campus battles against conservatives and communists. "You could never type him," Robert Wells, a campus friend and political compatriot, was to say years later. "He could meet whatever situation came up and it was already apparent that he was a problem solver rather than a person confined to ideology." Unruh lost two bids for the state Assembly but was elected on his third try in 1954 and came to the Capitol, taking to it like the proverbial duck to water. The young veteran's genius for political organization quickly made itself felt, and he caught a break with an appointment to the Finance and Insurance Committee that, for the first time, exposed him to the moneyed world of banking, one that the sharecropper's son soon adopted as his own. It led to a friendship with savings and loan tycoon Howard Ahmanson, who shepherded Unruh's political career and helped secure his personal financial situation as well. By the late 1950s, Unruh was a power. Changing the way business was done in the Capitol, he was well on his way to earning the nickname "Big Daddy" that he despised so much.

As summer heat enveloped Sacramento in 1960, an article appeared in *Reader's Digest,* purportedly a first-person account of how politics worked in the Capitol by "Assemblyman X" as told to Lester Velie, the investigative journalist whose *Collier's* magazine article about lobbyist Artie Samish 11 years earlier had started him on a downhill slide that ended in federal prison. The theme of the piece, was that while Samish was gone from the Capitol, his successors were conducting business pretty much in the same vein. Through Velie, the unnamed lawmaker described how he had come to Sacramento as an idealist bent on doing good and resisting the blandishments of lobbyists' offers of food, liquor, and entertainment but soon learned that to gain the power he needed to accomplish his legislative goals, he and like-minded legislators needed money to get allies elected and the only real source of such money was the corps of special interest lobbyists. "This is my dilemma," Assemblyman X told Velie. "If I had stayed away from the lobbyists I would have been ineffective. If I take their money and give them nothing for it, I am a cheat. If I do their bidding, I would be cheating the public. I find myself rationalizing what I have done. The tragedy is that I may wind up serving the very elements I set out to beat—yet, not even know that I have changed."

If there was a moral dilemma, the young assemblyman resolved it in favor of taking the lobbyists' money. "In the end," he said, "we found there was only one place where it could be had readily—from the third house itself. So stilling our doubts and scruples, we began to play the dangerous game of taking our money from would-be corrupters—to elect men who would fight corruption." Ultimately, Assemblyman X wrote, the strategy was successful in electing enough independent legislators that "We had broken the backbone of control from the outside."

James Mills, an Unruh lieutenant in the Assembly who later became president pro tem of the state Senate, wrote a book, *A Disorderly House,* about his old mentor many years later and said that the governor of the era, Pat Brown, told him that "Assemblyman X" was Unruh, and certainly the facts cited in the *Reader's Digest* article coincided with Unruh's rise to power in the Assembly, culminating in his election as speaker on his 39th birthday in 1961. Unruh himself more or less acknowledged his not-so-secret identity before his death. Until Unruh's rise to total power in the Assembly, lobbyists had continued to practice the "select and elect" strategy employed by Samish, controlling which candidates and parties would receive their favors based on their loyalty. But Unruh wanted to wrest control from lobbyists and create a powerful legislative leadership that would make its own decisions, for whatever motives, about who should be elected, and become the conduit for all-important campaign money. Over the next generation, as designed by Unruh and implemented by his successors—most notably Willie Brown—the system evolved from one driven by special interests and their lobbyists to one largely directed from within the Legislature itself with legislative leaders deciding how money was collected and spent. The advent of legislative term limits in the 1990s weakened that process and may have allowed lobbyists to reassert their previous primacy.

Unruh always contended that his actions, including the creation of a full-time Legislature and a much-expanded, professional staff, were directed at making lawmakers free of undue influence from the third house. It was an attitude

captured in Unruh's famous advice to young legislators about dealing with lobbyists: "If you can't eat their food, drink their booze, screw their women, take
their money and then vote against them, you've got no business being up here."
But critics contend that Unruh's overhaul of the Capitol was aimed at creating
an insular political class that was answerable to no one, sustained by a system-
atic shakedown of interest groups for money to keep the oligarchy in power. The
debate over Unruh's intentions and the results of what he wrought in Sacramento continues decades after he first achieved power and reverberates in such
developments as the imposition of term limits on legislators to prevent them
from spending too many years in the Capitol.

What's not debatable is that Unruh's election as speaker, the Supreme
Court's "one man, one vote" decision that shifted power in the state Senate from
rural areas to the cities, and voter approval of the full-time, professional Legislature in 1966 combined to radically change the way lobbyists conducted business
as they changed the makeup and the orientation of lawmakers themselves from
amateurs to political technocrats, a process that took roughly a decade to
achieve. By the mid-1970s, the change of climate had made itself felt. Unruh
himself was forced by political circumstances to take up residence in a new office, that of state treasurer, which he quickly built into a political and financial
powerhouse, using the billions of dollars in state budget and pension invest-
ments to impact national and even international financial markets and forcing
Wall Street bankers to do his bidding. By 1980, after a year-long bloodletting
among the Assembly's Democrats, one-time Unruh protégé Willie Brown—
another refugee from the poverty of rural Texas—had assumed the speakership,
bringing into power the student who was to outshine the teacher. Brown auda-
ciously took Unruh's system to new heights, centralizing control over the recruitment and financing of candidates, forcing special interests to funnel their
money either through his hands or those of trusted lieutenants, and brokering
backroom deals for the passage and defeat of legislation. In the view of many,
Tammany Hall had come to California—and it created a backlash that included
the federal investigation of influence peddling that snared Clay Jackson and
many others, and the imposition of term limits.

The major difference between Unruh and Brown was that the former never
lost sight of his policy goals as he accumulated power while the latter rarely
pursued any goals other than maintaining himself and his party in power. In fact,
one of Brown's moves during his speakership was to dismantle the professional,
apolitical staff that Unruh and his immediate successors had created and reorient
the staff to the political side of the legislative equation, using power over legislation to hammer the third house for campaign money. It's no accident that when
the FBI conducted its "sting" investigation of the Legislature during the late
1980s, agents focused as much on staffers as they did legislators themselves and
several were indicted and imprisoned.

While "Assemblyman X" had lamented about the need for campaign money to get like-minded politicians elected, the amounts of money involved in those elections was relatively small. It was not unusual for legislative candidates to spend only a few thousand dollars on campaigns until well into the 1960s. The first $100,000 Assembly campaign didn't appear until the early 1970s—and then only because partisan control of the house appeared to be at stake—and the first lobbyist-oriented Sacramento fundraising event was not staged until the late 1970s. But when Assembly Speaker Leo McCarthy and challenger Howard Berman conducted their year-long duel in 1980, both sides learned—much to their amazement at the time—that they could impose huge demands for money on special interests and their lobbyists and the demands would be met. Politicians also learned that the expanded reporting of campaign contributions imposed by Proposition 9 in 1974 provided them with a useful road map. They could see who was contributing to their partisan or factional rivals and demand parity, another escalator of campaign money collections and disbursements. Jerry Brown, running for the governorship in 1974 on a platform of political reform, had sponsored Proposition 9, which imposed a $10 monthly limit on lobbyists' goods and gifts to legislators—enough, Brown said, for two hamburgers and a Coke—and created a Fair Political Practices Commission to police the new law. One early decision faced by the commission was whether the mating of dogs owned by a lobbyist and a lawmaker was a prohibited transaction. More significantly, one provision of Proposition 9 barring lobbyists from making or arranging for campaign contributions was tossed out by the courts as an abridgement of free speech.

The flow of legislative campaign money escalated through the 1980s, finally approaching $100 million during every two years or about $1 million per legislative seat. Campaign "events"—breakfasts, lunches, dinners, fishing trips, golf tournaments, baseball outings, etc.—were staged by the hundreds, both in Sacramento and other locales with the goal of raising from $25,000 to $250,000 each time. The pressure to give became so intense that even lobbyists complained, albeit privately, about the system evolving into what one described as "an abysmal shakedown" in which the passage or rejection of legislation had become a virtual auction. Speaker Brown made it clear to lobbyists that he expected to control a large percentage of their campaign budgets, either directly through contributions to him and his lieutenants, or indirectly by dictating a recipient. And it was not uncommon for issues to be kept alive year after year to milk the principals for campaign contributions and, some believed, lobbying fees. The years-long conflict over how California would tax multinational corporations, largely financed by Japanese corporations, is often cited by Capitol insiders as one legislative cow that was milked by everyone involved—resolved only when the Japanese finally concluded that they were being played for suckers and demanded that the issue be decided one way or the other. It's not unknown for legislators, sometimes in league with lobbyists, to push legislation specifically to attract campaign contributions and/or lobbying fees, although the practice is considered to be a breach of ethics in both professions.

By the late 1980s, and especially after the FBI's sting resulted in indictments of legislators, lobbyists, and staffers, there was a crescendo of demands for reform, such as the imposition of contribution and/or spending limits, and voters passed several measures, only to see them invalidated by the courts on free speech grounds. The only lasting changes resulting from the scandal were the measure to impose term limits, three two-year terms in the Assembly and two four-year terms in the Senate, and a legislatively generated law that barred lawmakers from taking "honoraria"—speaking fees or some facsimile thereof that had played such a large role in the FBI-monitored bribery of Capitol denizens—and creating a commission that sharply raised legislators' salaries. Term limits forced Willie Brown out of the Assembly and into the San Francisco mayor's office, and Brown's long tenure was followed by a succession of brief and much weaker speakerships. Not surprisingly, the Brown mayoral regime has been plagued by allegations of influence peddling on land development and other matters and a succession of journalistic and official investigations into the allegations. Several lobbyists who had worked the Capitol based on their connections to Brown during his speakership set up branch offices in San Francisco and collected new clients who needed access to city hall.

Through all of these changes, the number of lobbyists in Sacramento and the interest groups employing them both grew rapidly, even as the manner in which they operated evolved. The growth stemmed from three developments that had the collective effect of increasing the role that state government was playing in the daily lives of Californians and their corporations, labor unions, professional organizations, and local governments. One was that California's economy was changing rapidly, moving from the industrialism that arose during and after World War II to a postindustrial mode involving services, such as medical care, and high technology. The evolution of medical care as California's largest single economic activity, for instance, created a huge corps of trade organizations and lobbyists specializing in medical issues. Trade associations doubled, tripled, and then quadrupled in size, and many fragmented along specialized interest lines, each requiring its own lobbying structure. And even as corporations or other interests maintained their membership in umbrella organizations, many dispatched their own lobbyists to Sacramento, or hired contract lobbyists, to pursue their even narrower goals.

Another factor was Proposition 13, the 1978 ballot measure that sharply reduced and limited local property taxes and shifted primary responsibility for financing schools and local governments, particularly counties, to Sacramento. That broke down the once-strong wall that had existed between special interest lobbying by the liquor and other groups and broader public policy matters, such as schools and highways. Suddenly, the field of interest groups was expanded dramatically as school officials, teacher unions, mayors, county supervisors, and other once-remote figures scrambled for money in Sacramento, and all of them needed lobbyists.

The third development was a wave of regulatory activism that had begun during the Pat Brown-Jesse Unruh era in the 1960s and continued to build even during Republican governorships (Ronald Reagan, for instance, signed the California Environmental Quality Act). While the new regulations were supposed to create more social and economic fairness and protect the public's health and environment, the darker side of liberal government is that every new regulatory program creates, quite naturally, one or more interest groups that want to affect regulatory policies, whether by legislation or administrative decree, and each group needs someone to represent it in the halls of government. Some of the new regulations were sought by special interest groups themselves to gain advantages over competitors, such as the late-blooming effort in 1999 by grocery store chains and their unions to block "big box" retailers from selling groceries.

A prime, but by no means solitary, example of how regulation begets lobbying activity is what happened after voters, in 1972, passed an environmentalist-sponsored initiative to impose development controls along the 1,000-mile-long California coastline, to be administered by a new Coastal Commission. The implementing legislation, enacted several years later, allowed eight of the 12 seats on the new commission to be filled by legislative leaders and just four by the governor—and all of them served at the pleasure of the appointing power, which meant that they could be fired instantaneously if they didn't do what their political masters wanted. The legislation also specified a "coastal zone" in which development came under control of the commission.

Overnight, the controls created an incentive for landowners and developers to influence what properties could be developed. Indeed, the existence of the controls themselves made developable land inside the coastal zone more valuable, raising the economic stakes even further. Immediately, there arose a corps of lobbyists who said they could, through their influence with legislative leaders, get projects cleared for development and/or get legislation passed that exempted certain parcels from the coastal zone and thus Coastal Commission purview.

One example of the syndrome occurred in northern San Diego County in the mid-1980s when a development consulting firm organized local coastal landowners to contribute money to a drive to enact legislation exempting 4,000 acres of land from coastal zone protections, thereby making the property easier to sell or develop. "Remember (the) benefit to your property would increase at least $10,000–$15,000 (per acre) should SB1808 be successful," the solicitation said. The organizers said that getting the measure enacted would cost about $400,000—for lobbying fees and campaign contributions primarily—or $100 per acre, thus offering a return on the political investment of at least 100–1. Bernard Teitelbaum, a lobbyist who specialized in coastal zone cases, wanted $74,000 for his services and another $100,000-plus was budgeted for campaign contributions—graphic evidence that interest groups and their lobbyists see a need to buy access.

A few years after that case played itself out, in what many observers believe to have been only the tip of a very forbidding iceberg, one coastal commissioner was clapped in federal prison for soliciting bribes from landowners. (It's well known in the Capitol that a high-level Senate staff member talked a big land development company into giving him $50,000 in cash to be distributed as bribes to legislators to get a coastal zone exemption for the company's Southern California land enacted, but that the staffer pocketed the money and then dared the developer to complain to authorities. The case was investigated by the FBI but no charges were brought because of a lack of hard evidence.) Whether coastal development controls have been good or bad in the larger sense, there's no question that they have generated millions of dollars in fees for lobbyists.

The coastal act's experience was mirrored in dozens of other regulatory areas, such as pesticide registration, water quality, consumer protection, medical care, air pollution, construction standards, and labor relations. And as the regulatory programs proliferated, lobbyists often found themselves dealing with administrative agencies, charged with implementing and enforcing the new laws, as well as the Legislature. The lobbyists themselves came under regulation with the adoption of Proposition 9 in 1974 and formed their own lobbying organization, the Institute of Governmental Advocates, to represent their interests with the Fair Political Practices Commission and in the Legislature. The partial shift of lobbying focus from the Legislature to administrative agencies and their power to issue regulations with the force of law came to a head in the late 1970s when business executives began complaining about the liberal activists who filled many of the slots in Jerry Brown's administration and began issuing regulations that the businessmen saw as onerous, arbitrary, and unreflective of the underlying legislation. A coalition of business lobbyists began pushing legislation that would allow the Legislature to review and reject administrative regulations. It was on the verge of success when then-Assembly Speaker Leo McCarthy devised a compromise that would create an Office of Administrative Law to review administrative regulations for compliance with law. In doing so, he inadvertently created still another layer of regulatory bureaucracy for lobbyists to work on behalf of their clients.

As the 20th century came to a close, lobbying was still a growing trade in Sacramento. Its culture had changed dramatically, becoming more professional, its practitioners had become a much broader group, including more women and ethnic minorities, and its techniques had evolved with the advent of term limits, which mandated a constant turnover of legislators and staffers. But its essential purposes remained as intact as they were during Southern Pacific's heyday or the Artie Samish era—to influence government policy in ways that benefit or protect the lobbyists' clients.

Four decades after Samish's reign had ended, a former state legislator who had become a lobbyist, John Quimby, was delivering a guest lecture to a graduate class in political science at the University of California, Davis, a few miles west of the Capitol, when a student posed a question: "Sir, would you shed some light on something I've always wondered about? Suppose you find that your personal views are 180 degrees different from the interests of your clients. As you undertake to lobby the issue, how do you go about reconciling the differences in your mind?"

Without a moment's hesitation, Quimby delivered a reply that was only half-facetious and captured the detached attitude of the professional Sacramento lobbyist: "I simply keep increasing my fee until the conflict disappears."

CHAPTER 2

Who Hires Lobbyists, and Why?

"No man's life, liberty or property are safe while the Legislature is in session."—J. Gideon Tucker

Al Wickland didn't know he needed a lobbyist until one day in 1982 when he learned—quite by chance, he says—that a much larger competitor was using its political pull to damage his business. Wickland Oil was a relatively small but thriving wholesale and retail petroleum products business, headquartered just a few miles from the Capitol, operating several dozen gasoline stations itself and supplying gasoline to other independent dealers in northern California. Its primary competition in the latter trade was Tosco, a huge but little-known gasoline refiner that didn't sell gasoline directly to the public but was a major supplier of fuel to independent stations in the state.

Wickland had been a Tosco customer itself but had become a direct competitor when it constructed a terminal on the Carquinez Strait and began receiving tanker shipments of gasoline from China, which it then blended with lead to meet California's higher octane requirements—these being the days before leaded gasoline was banned altogether. At the time, the state Air Resources Board maintained different lead content standards for large refiners such as Tosco and small refiners. Wickland executives assumed that their blending operations fell under the small refinery rules and operated accordingly.

What Al Wickland learned one day was that Tosco's lobbyists were trying to write language into an already active piece of legislation that would have the practical effect of putting Wickland's new blending operation out of business by imposing on blenders the same lead standards as those applied by the Air Resources Board to large refiners. While nothing official had appeared in print, typewritten copies of the proposed language—just a few words—were circulating in the Capitol, and it was planned to insert the words into a measure then pending in a two-house "conference committee," a process that requires explanation for those not familiar with the Capitol's often-arcane ways.

Legislators make much of the "committee process," in which raw legislation is shaped into acceptable form—or rejected—by subjecting it to hearings, discussions, debates, and negotiations in policy committees, which deal with specific subject areas, or the appropriations committees of both houses, through which every major piece of legislation must pass. In theory, this process is public and participatory; in practice, much of what happens is decided by principal parties, including lobbyists, in private and then simply unveiled in the public setting. But at least there's that much exposure, including analyses of the bills by committee staffs, that provide a modicum of explanation in everyday language of what's happening.

But even minimal public exposure is too much for some legislation, what some term "mushroom bills" because they can only thrive in dark and dank places. These measures are such blatant grabs for power, money, or both that they can only be enacted if virtually no one knows they exist, often comprising just a few cryptic words inserted into some much-larger piece of legislation without any explanation as to the true effect. Slipping such legislation through the process and into law is called "low-balling" and until some procedural reforms dampened their use, two-house conference committees were a much-used and much-abused vehicle for this low-profile legislating. Indeed, some legislators and some lobbyists are known as "low-ball artists" for their wizardry in the technique.

A conference committee, usually three members from each legislative house, supposedly resolves conflicts between competing Senate and Assembly versions of similar legislation, and it occasionally rises to that lofty purpose. The annually convened conference committee that writes a final version of the state budget is one example. More often, however, a conference committee is used to amend, or even completely rewrite, legislation without its having to go through the formal committee process of hearings, analyses, and votes. A bill can be "taken into conference" by a simple floor vote of one house rejecting amendments approved in the other house, usually done at the behest of the bill's author, and that—until reforms were enacted in the late 1980s—meant that the author could substantially change the measure and bring it to the floors of both houses for quick passage with little, if any, public notice or exposure.

Once, it was not unusual to have dozens of bills "in conference" at one time, usually in the last, frantic days of a legislative session, and all could become vehicles for legislation that had never been seen or heard in a regular committee. It was common, in fact, for conference committees never to have public meetings, but for the drafter of the revised legislation to simply have committee members sign their names on a "conference committee report," the final version of the legislation, perhaps without even knowing its contents. Stories abound in the Capitol about how conference committees were used to do this or that in the dead of night, with only a few insiders watching or knowing what was happening, hinged on the truism that few legislators ever read the bills on which they are voting. And that's exactly what Tosco and its agents would have done to upstart competitor Wickland Oil had Al Wickland not learned of the maneuver and quickly hired a lobbyist.

The lobbyist Wickland retained is a good one, former FBI agent, former cattle trader and former state Senator Dennis Carpenter, an affable Republican who nevertheless is popular among the Capitol's Democrats and whose new lobbying firm was already establishing itself as one of Sacramento's top players when Wickland signed on. As soon as Carpenter entered the picture, it evolved into a very messy and very public high-stakes affair.

Both sides employed all of the tricks of modern lobbying—personal calls on legislators, public relations and media barrages, and alliances with organizations that could sway public and/or legislative opinion—and focused them on the six members of the conference committee headed by the late Assemblyman Walter Ingalls, an acerbic Riverside County Democrat who had agreed to front the issue for Tosco's agents. Tosco teamed up with other independent refiners, refinery worker unions and environmental groups, contending that the pending legislation—which still hadn't been put in any official form—would close what they called a "loophole" that blenders such as Wickland enjoyed and would reduce the amount of lead emissions into the atmosphere. Some of the Tosco coalition's propaganda hinted darkly about the exporting of jobs from American refineries to communist China. Wickland countered by charging that the Tosco amendment was designed simply to choke off competition in supplying gasoline to independent service stations and thus pad Tosco's profits—and Wickland scored a public relations coup when it proved that Tosco itself had been importing gasoline from China.

As the propaganda war escalated, Ingalls was forced to schedule an open conference committee meeting, and the lobbyists for both sides zeroed in on the committee members. "We're up here in force today," a Tosco public relations operative crowed one day as the firm fielded a large team of executives and lobbyists to prowl Capitol hallways. "We've got Denny Carpenter over there doing likewise," said Wickland's field general, lawyer Dan Hall. When Ingalls scheduled the meeting, it appeared that he and Tosco had the four votes—at least two from each house—required to produce a conference committee report, but Carpenter's efforts had softened support and Ingalls was compelled to postpone the meeting, buying more time for Wickland.

As it happened, the Tosco-Wickland duel ended on a whimper, not a bang. There never was a showdown vote in the conference committee or on the legislative floors in 1982. When a newspaper reporter revealed that Mickey Kantor, a prominent member of then-Gov. Jerry Brown's political inner circle, was pushing the Tosco bill and had arranged for a Tosco contribution to Brown's 1982 campaign for the U.S. Senate, Brown went ballistic and ordered Kantor and Ingalls to drop the matter altogether. It would have been embarrassing for Brown to have the Tosco bill land on his desk under the circumstances. Wickland, meanwhile, realized that he had dodged a political bullet that, if it had found its mark, would have cost him millions of dollars. And for many years thereafter, he kept Carpenter's lobbying firm on retainer to guard against a repeat.

As important as it may have been to Wickland, and presumably to Tosco, their 1982 clash was not an unusual one. Hundreds of times each year, situations arise in the Capitol that could have heavy consequences for those affected. And that, in the broadest sense, is why thousands of corporations, unions, trade associations, ideological groups, and local governments employ lobbyists. In fact, assuming that every Californian lives in and pays taxes to at least one local government jurisdiction—and most live in several—it could be said that no Californian is not paying for professional representation in Sacramento on some issue, even if he or she is unaware of it.

The most prolific employer of lobbyists to influence governmental decision making is, in fact, government itself. Reports compiled by the secretary of state's office covering lobbying activities during 1999 and 2000 indicate that government agencies, mostly cities and counties, spent $52.9 million on lobbying—about 15 percent of the $344.3 million total and over $9 million more than the second largest category, health care. And school-related entities, including school districts, spent several million dollars more, expanding the role of government lobbying even further.

To those inside the Capitol, it's not surprising that governments are major users of lobbyists, not only their own employees but high-priced contract lobbyists, because they're jousting over many billions of dollars, often in competition with one another. While local governments and schools had used lobbyists for decades, mostly to secure more financial aid from Sacramento, the enactment of Proposition 13 in 1978 raised the stakes immensely by making the state the primary source of funds for local agencies. Proposition 13 slashed local property taxes by more than 50 percent and imposed strict limits on their future growth. Within weeks of its enactment, Governor Jerry Brown and the Legislature had appropriated billions of dollars for what was known as a "bailout" that became a permanent shift of financial responsibility for schools and local services to Sacramento. Elementary and high schools alone now consume about 40 percent of the state's general fund budget and when subventions to local governments are counted, the total stakes easily surpass $50 billion a year, big money in anyone's language and well worth an investment in lobbying.

The scramble for state money is heightened by the way—or the many ways—it's distributed. Rather than simply transfer funds to schools and local governments—particularly counties—in large blocs and allow the dollars to be spent by locally elected school boards, county boards of supervisors, and city councils, the governor and the Legislature have created dozens of specific aid programs, each with its own set of operating criteria and each, supposedly, designed to accomplish some specific purpose. That means that in addition to the dollars themselves, government lobbyists dicker and squabble constantly over the rules governing their distribution, which can significantly increase or decrease what any one government entity receives. And the micromanagement has become more complicated as the amounts of money have increased—in part because legislators could use the financial leverage to compel local officials to operate the way lawmakers wanted on issues disconnected from the aid packages themselves. Thus, for example, legislators from huge Los Angeles County could become, albeit indirectly, powers in local affairs through their control of the pursestrings. One of many examples: Los Angeles legislators used a threat to withhold state money to compel the Los Angeles County Board of Supervisors to build a public hospital much larger than the supervisors considered prudent, delaying construction for years until a compromise deal was brokered on the final day of the 2000 legislative session. Beyond money, too, local government and school lobbyists often find themselves involved in such issues as classroom instruction content, pupil testing, teacher competency standards, land-use policies, redevelopment, transportation, and water.

Virtually every city, county, and school district bigger than a gnat maintains a lobbying presence in Sacramento, along with the larger special purpose districts, such as the Metropolitan Water District of Southern California, which was spending over $100,000 a month on lobbying in 2000. And there are dozens of governmental consortia, ranging from the all-purpose ones such as the League of California Cities, the California State Association of Counties, and the California School Boards Association, to the smaller, narrowly focused groups. Many of the latter emerged due to the entrepreneurial spirit of lobbyists who, emulating pioneer lobbyist Artie Samish, recruited local governments and school districts that had interests in common and created their own specialized subgroups, based on the quirks they saw in the post-Proposition 13 array of state financial aid. Thus, for example, were born lobbies such as the Association for Low Wealth Schools and the California Association of Suburban School Districts, the Regional Council of Rural Counties and the Tri-Valley Alliance of Recreation and Park Districts. The dozens of governmental lobbying organizations registered with the secretary of state's office, incidentally, include some foreign governments and some Indian tribes, especially those which operate gambling casinos, and which, unlike other governments, are lavish contributors to politicians' campaigns.

In the main, government lobbyists operate much like their brethren in the private sector, although they lack one important tool—campaign contributions. But one reason why many governments prefer to use expensive contract lobbyists, rather than their own employees, is that the contractors often make or arrange for campaign contributions on behalf of their private clients, thus gaining access and stature that can benefit their governmental clients. Hustling public-sector lobbyists also make up for their lack of campaign contributions by forming alliances with interest groups, such as unions representing teachers and local government workers, that do parcel out campaign money. When several groups combine forces, they will sometimes form semiformal "communities," as they call themselves, and thus focus their energies on an issue and protect themselves from being divided and conquered by politicians and rival interests. One reason why the "education coalition" has been so consistently successful in securing more money for public schools is that it used the campaign money of the California Teachers Association. Local governments have been hammered repeatedly in Sacramento's wars over budget allocations because they have been unable to replicate that pattern. Indeed, local governments and their unions often find themselves sparring in Sacramento over such matters as binding arbitration rather than cooperating toward a common goal.

An anecdote that illustrates the world of the public-sector lobbyist: Ray Corley, a specialist in water matters, was working for the City of Los Angeles in the late 1970s and early 1980s when the Legislature was dealing with highly controversial legislation to build a Peripheral Canal around the Sacramento-San Joaquin Delta and deliver more northern California water to southern California. At one point, the fate of the legislation was in the hands of the Senate's water committee, which had scheduled a late-evening hearing and vote, and everyone involved knew it would come down to one Los Angeles senator who was a well-known drunk and unlikely to show up at the hearing on his own, or at least in any state of sobriety. Corley was assigned by Los Angeles city officials to babysit the wayward senator throughout the day and make sure he showed up at the hearing sober enough to vote. What ensued was a comic opera episode that still draws chuckles when recounted among Capitol insiders. Corley got the senator to the hearing but could use his hulking presence to guard just one of the hearing room's two doors and as the hearing droned on, the senator was clearly getting nervous, periodically telling his colleagues that he would leave if the vote was not taken soon. The opponents of the bill slowed down their debate, deliberately provoking the senator to leave—and at one point he fled through the unguarded door with Corley in full pursuit. The lobbyist followed his charge across to a bar across the street and allowed him to have a couple of drinks to settle his nerves, then pulled him back to the hearing room where, eventually and after much confusion, he voted for the Peripheral Canal bill. Corley did his job that night, and eventually the Peripheral Canal was approved by the Legislature, although it was rejected by the state's voters in a subsequent referendum election and was never built.

A quirky sidelight to the major, even dominant, role that local governments play in the employment of lobbyists emerged in 2001, when veteran advocate Donald K. BrOwn—known as "Big O" for the unusual spelling of his name—

was fined $32,000 by the Fair Political Practices Commission for laundering, or failing to report, a series of campaign contributions in 1996 to two city council candidates in Chula Vista, a small city south of San Diego, near the Mexican border. Why would one of the Capitol's most influential lobbyists engage in laundering donations, using members of his own family, to get around Chula Vista's limit on individual donations? The investigation suggested that it had much to do with the fact that BrOwn's lobbying firm, Advocation Inc., held a contract to represent the city in Sacramento and wanted to ensure that the contract was maintained.

If government, including schools, is, in financial terms, the biggest employer of lobbyists, the other powerhouses are business organizations with a direct stake in state regulation, such as health care, banking, insurance, and utilities. But while financial and utility interests are old-timers around the Capitol, the emergence of health care as a major political battleground, and thus a source of business for Capitol lobbyists, is a relatively recent phenomenon, stemming directly from the conversion of California's economy during the last generation, from one centered on resources and manufacturing to one dominated by services and trade. Health care is now California's largest single industry, accounting for at least 10 percent of the state's $1.3 trillion economy, and is several times as large as any other major sector, such as agriculture, entertainment, high technology, and aerospace. The huge amounts of money involved in health care, its preoccupying place in the consciousness of the public, the emotional impact of specific health issues, and the evident willingness of health care factions to make lavish campaign contributions combine to raise its political profile to the highest levels.

No legislative session is complete without at least one battle—and usually several—over health care. They include the perennial struggles between medical care providers and personal injury lawyers, turf wars among medical specialties on which procedures can be legally performed on patients, duels over the allocation of health care dollars, and, most recently, conflicts between powerful, multibillion-dollar health maintenance organizations (HMOs) and their critics over regulation of the burgeoning HMO industry. And while one could write a book devoted to medical care clashes in the Capitol, one stands out as being both emblematic of the syndrome and highly colorful unto itself: the great war over who could perform surgery on the ankle.

As participatory baby boomer sports such as tennis, skiing, and running became popular in the 1970s, doctors and hospitals began experiencing an upsurge in ankle injuries, some of which required surgery. And under state law that delineates which medical procedures can be performed by which licensed health care provider, only medical doctors—usually orthopedic surgeons—could operate on ankles, a fact underscored by an attorney general's opinion. But podiatrists, whose field was legally restricted to the foot below the ankle, wanted to move up the leg. For years, the podiatrists' lobbying group had sponsored bills to expand their scope of practice upward, some as far as the hip. But just as regularly, lobbyists for the California Medical Association had beaten back the attempts. Finally, in the early 1980s, the podiatrists' lobbyist, Bob Walters (no relation to the co-author of this book despite their physical resemblance and a widespread Capitol belief that they are brothers or cousins), told his clients after another setback that to win their struggle, they'd have to take the game more seriously, limit their aspirations to the ankle, raise a substantial amount of campaign money, and distribute it assiduously around the Capitol, beginning with the all-powerful Speaker of the Assembly, Willie Brown. The foot doctors took Walters' advice, put together a warchest of about $150,000 and set to work.

Over several months, with the ankle surgery bill having been "speakerized," it sailed over the Assembly's hurdles one by one with the podiatrists and their lobbyist contending that it was a safe and natural extension of their scope of practice. "We always considered the foot and the ankle as one entity," the California Podiatry Association's executive director, Dr. Robert Johns, said after the battle was over. "We have no desire to move up the leg."

With Brown's support, Assembly approval was a dead certainty. The Senate became the battleground, and lobbyists for the podiatrists and the orthopedic surgeons ("pods vs. orthopods" in Capitol shorthand) zeroed in on a key factor: which Senate committee would handle the measure. Theoretically, it could have gone to either the Senate Health and Welfare Committee or the Senate Business and Professions Committee. The podiatrists wanted it in the former, believing it to have a friendlier membership, while California Medical Association lobbyists preferred the latter. But when it came before the Senate Rules Committee for a decision, the Health and Welfare Committee's chairwoman was granted her request for jurisdiction while the Business and Professions Committee chairman, oddly enough, did not even ask for the bill to be placed under his purview. After that major setback, CMA lobbyists were able to win a couple of preliminary votes in the Senate but eventually the bill was approved and signed into law, a huge win for the podiatrists and an unusual setback for the CMA. The news media had a field day with the issue since there's something inherently funny about fighting over the foot. When the podiatrists' lost one skirmish in the Senate, one reporter wrote, tongue in cheek, that they had suffered "the agony of defeat." But it was serious business to the interest groups involved and their lobbyists.

The skill and persistence of the foot doctors and their lobbyist and the credibility of the legislator carrying the bill, a registered nurse, in assuring colleagues that the measure presented no medical peril both played roles in the outcome—a posture underscored by the podiatrists' recruitment of medical doctors to testify at committee hearings. But the campaign warchest also played a substantial part in the ankle drama. A newspaper reporter later compiled an extensive examination of contributions and votes on the bill and found a high correlation between dates on the podiatrists' checks and favorable votes. One of those receiving a big podiatrist check was Sen. Joseph Montoya, the Business and

Professions Committee chairman who had not requested jurisdiction on the bill and who some years later was sent to federal prison for taking bribes in the FBI's undercover investigation of Capitol corruption. Montoya never cast one vote on the podiatrists' measure, his disinterest being the important factor. Dr. Johns said later that it was necessary to weigh in with campaign contributions because the CMA was "one of the biggest spenders in the Legislature," adding, "I think we got the attention of the Legislature. Look at the people who voted for us and look who we supported."

A year after the pods had defeated the orthopods, the CMA lobbyist, talking with the podiatry association leaders, told them he had no regrets because, "You bought it fair and square." Even so, how did the podiatrists' money make an impact when it was still a tiny fraction of the campaign funds that the CMA distributed every year? Because it was concentrated on one issue. The CMA tracks dozens, even hundreds, of bills in each legislative session and in the broader array of medical issues, the podiatrists' bill was fairly minor, of importance to a relative handful of CMA physician-members. Legislators concluded—with encouragement from the podiatrists—that they could vote with the foot doctors on this one issue that was of paramount importance to them and make it up to the CMA on other issues more important to the big medical lobby.

It illustrated the weakness of large, multi-issue organizations when confronted by a highly focused drive by a much smaller group—a weakness that other small interest groups have exploited on other matters, essentially adapting the theories of insurgency warfare to the political arena. And it explains why there has been a distinct tendency for interest groups in all fields to fragment into more concentrated subgroups, sometimes at the behest of lobbyists who see a vacuum and fill it. Not surprisingly, in the aftermath of the podiatry bill's success, several other specialized medical lobbies were formed to wage war the perennial "scope of practice" conflict. In 2000, optometrists and ophthalmologists, who had long battled over eye care issues, agreed on scope of practice guidelines and found themselves battling the California Medical Association, which disliked the idea of an end run. But the eye care coalition saw its legislation enacted anyway.

The most humorous of the scope of practice clashes may have been a battle between veterinarians and dog groomers over who had the legal right to brush dogs' teeth and another between doctors and trendy "colonic clinics" over whether the latter's business of administering enemas to clean out clients' bowels constituted practicing medicine without a license.

Everyone in the Capitol expects that health care will continue to be a growth sector for the lobbying corps as it occupies an ever-larger role in the economy and the public consciousness. One major 21st-century issue will be the widening divide between those with and without health care coverage; at the turn of the century, more than seven million Californians lacked coverage and expanding coverage, as medical providers were urging, could cost billions of

dollars a year. And health issues—availability and price of care and HMO regulation particularly—will be a preoccupation of the state's affluent, rapidly aging
and politically influential baby boom generation. A strong signal of health care's
political maturation is that the legislative committees dealing with health issues,
once considered Capitol backwaters, have become "juice committees," Capitol's
parlance for committees whose issues generate not only lobbying fees but campaign contributions, and thus are highly desired plums for legislative leaders to
award to the faithful.

Interestingly, however, not everyone coming to the Capitol with a legislative goal wants to hire a lobbyist. In the mid-1980s, an informal organization of
catalog printers from the San Fernando Valley persuaded a local legislator to
carry a bill that would exempt catalogs produced for big mail order retailers
from the state sales tax, arguing that catalogs produced in other states were not
taxed, thus creating a competitive disadvantage for the Californians. The
amounts of tax money involved were relatively small, Governor George Deukmejian's administration was supporting the bill as an economic development
incentive and there was no opposition. The bill sailed through the Assembly
without dissent and moved quickly through its initial Senate committee only to
be stalled in a second committee whose chairman refused to schedule a hearing.
Finally, the chairman's aide bluntly told the printers that for the bill to move,
they had to hire a specific lobbyist and pay him $30,000.

The printers angrily rejected what they regarded as an extortion attempt and
as threatened, the bill was killed without a vote. The printers complained to the
Federal Bureau of Investigation, which dispatched a couple of agents to the
Capitol to interview the principals. The FBI agents concluded that without a
paper trail, the case amounted to one person's word against another although
they believed that the printers were telling the truth and the senator was lying
when he insisted that he blocked the bill to avoid punching a special interest
loophole in the state tax laws. The case was never pursued, and one agent told a
journalist that "it will take a sting to crack this place" because conventional investigative techniques couldn't penetrate the Capitol's clubby culture in which
deals are done verbally with little or nothing committed to writing. A few years
later, the committee chairman retired and took up lobbying in partnership with
his one-time aide. The senator retired after the FBI took the wraps off its years-
long sting investigation of Capitol bribery that sent several politicians, legislative staffers, and lobbyists to federal prison. The printing tax break case may not
have directly inspired the FBI's undercover investigation, but the FBI agent's
comment was prophetic.

How interest groups recruit and pay lobbyists are two of the Capitol's more
arcane topics, as are such matters as whether lobbyists should be employees or
contractors and whether they should be on long-term contract through retainers
or hired as needed. The only constants are that lobbyists are well-paid—except,
perhaps, those who labor for nonprofit groups pursuing what they regard as is-

sues of conscience—and that every possible arrangement is found among the hundreds of lobbyists and the thousands of clients and employers. Most of the $344.3 million that interest groups reported spending on lobbying activities during the 1999–2000 biennial legislative session went for fees and salaries. And the 10 top-grossing lobbying operations reported nearly $49 million in income, an average of more than $4.8 million each, topped by the $8.5 million raked in by Kahl/Pownall Associates, a 13-lobbyist power center that reported having 60 clients, an eclectic mix that included oil companies, real estate developers, utilities, financial houses and, of course, a flock of health care firms. Partners Mike Kahl and Fred Pownall employ an experienced staff that includes former top administration officials and legislative staffers. Among other top-grossing lobbying operations are those headed by former Assemblyman Richard Robinson, the aforementioned Dennis Carpenter, former Deukmejian administration chief of staff Steve Merksamer, former high-ranking state Senate staffer Jerry Zanelli, and Aaron Read, who cut his teeth representing state employee unions but saw his clientele expand sharply with the election of Gray Davis as governor in 1998. Many of Read's union clients were early Davis endorsers, giving him special standing in the administration.

Insider knowledge and connections don't come cheap, as the gross incomes of the top lobbying firms imply. A full-service contract with a major firm can cost a client several hundred thousand dollars a year and maintaining one's own staff lobbyist can, with ancillary expenses, be just as expensive—although the costs still pale in comparison with the monetary stakes involved in most issues. Simple monitoring contracts can cost about $20,000 a year, and the average lobbying contract probably runs $5,000–7,000 a month. For that level of fee, a client can expect professional review and monitoring of legislation and regulations affecting his interests, and personal representation on perhaps a half-dozen specific bills or proposed regulations—roughly 15–20 percent of a lobbyist's working time. Occasionally, lobbyists are engaged for short periods—sometimes just one day—to help pass or kill a single bill, and that intense period of legislative firefighting can cost $25,000 to $50,000. It's a technique employed when a lobbyist is believed to have a unique relationship with one legislator whose vote is crucial to the outcome of the fight or a governor who has the bill sitting on his desk, awaiting a signature or a veto.

As the list of top lobbying firms implies, the Capitol's most influential advocates are usually men and women who have acquired experience and contacts on the public payroll and then segued into the private sector—emulating the prototypical Sacramento lobbyist, Artie Samish, who entered the field low-level clerical jobs in San Francisco city government and in the Legislature. At least a few dozen of Sacramento's 1,200-plus lobbyists are ex-legislators themselves, such as Carpenter and Robinson, who have left the Legislature but retain their lifetime memberships in the fraternity, who can understand and commiserate with contemporary lawmakers, who know the Capitol's secret rituals and rules as well as its formal procedures, who may be well-versed in a particular subject area, and who, of course, know which interest groups may need help with their political problems. In general, an ex-legislator's party affiliation is not an impediment to taking up lobbying, unless one is foolish enough to continue pursuing partisan causes after making the career switch. Personality transcends party in the fraternal atmosphere of the building.

Former legislative staffers make up an even larger segment of the lobbying community and what's true of ex-legislators is largely true of the former legislative employees as well; indeed, a substantial number of ex-legislators who take up lobbying are ex-staffers, that being the single largest occupational group in the Legislature prior to the advent of term limits. Some staffers who have concentrated in a single subject area while on the official payroll, particularly if that subject is a complex one, such as utility regulation or insurance, become so knowledgeable that their expertise is virtually priceless. Their conversion is seamless since they're dealing with precisely the same people and issues, just moving to another side of the table. These technical experts often find themselves dealing with state agencies as much as the Legislature since the agencies often implement the details of what the Legislature has wrought in broad policy, and the ability to speak the language of an issue is a valuable talent.

Men and women who fill high positions in a gubernatorial administration often gain the same kind of knowledge and contacts that ex-legislators and legislative staffers acquire, and they just as often move into private lobbying to cash in on their experience, such as Merksamer and former Ronald Reagan aide George Steffes. A few months before any governor leaves office, it's common for the upper ranks of his personal staff to thin out as aides find new careers, often in lobbying. And if the governor is replaced by someone from the same party, there's usually enough carryover for the ex-gubernatorial staffers to enjoy—and profit from—a higher level of access than other lobbyists could hope to have. Senior-level bureaucrats sometimes move into lobbying, especially when they are hired to deal with old friends in state agencies on regulatory matters.

There's a one-year prohibition on "revolving door" contacts involving ex-legislators, ex-legislative and gubernatorial staffers, and ex-bureaucrats, but it's not a serious impediment to career-switching. It's only a year and even without making direct contacts, the ex-somethings can still be effective as advisers to their clients while waiting for the period to end. And they can lobby entities not on the restricted list. One ploy often used by and for ex-legislators is to establish themselves as the head of a trade association that employs lobbyists. The ex-lawmaker may not even become a registered lobbyist but can continue to socialize—even claiming the privilege of ex-lawmakers to walk onto the floor of the legislative houses and schmooze—while implicitly representing their clients. A substantial number of lobbyists are lawyers, reflecting the fact that the two fields of advocacy share many similarities and that it doesn't hurt to have a law degree when writing law. And then there are people who just drift into the field, per-haps having been assigned to deal with legislation by their employers, and find it to their liking. For some, the attraction—beyond the high pay—is simply that it's an ever-changing, highly competitive game.

Still another subgroup of ex-somethings are former political campaign aides who move into lobbying when their candidates win, taking advantage of the connections they have with the new officeholder. It's an inside track that usually has only limited utility in the Legislature, since there are so many legislators and first-termers generally have little clout, although veteran Democratic campaign consultant Richie Ross carved out a lucrative sideline in lobbying. The cam-paign route to lobbying does mean something when a new governor takes office and some of his campaign aides hang out their shingles as lobbyists, advertising themselves as having free access to "the horseshoe," as Capitol types call the governor's suite of offices in the Capitol's southeastern corner, where top ad-ministration officials make policy that can have every bit as much impact as anything the Legislature does. Getting inside the horseshoe on a regular basis—particularly having the ability to be buzzed in by the receptionist without secu-rity clearance—is worth its weight in gold to a lobbyist and often, those with previous service to the incumbent governor have the inside track. One example popped up in 1999, when Davis became the state's first Democratic governor in 16 years and a young aide—who had also worked with Davis' wife, Sharon, at a private foundation—opened shop as a lobbyist after finishing his final political assignment for Davis, managing the new governor's inaugural celebration. The former aide, Darius Anderson, prospered as business and professional interests decided it wouldn't hurt to have someone on first-name terms with the new gov-ernor and his wife on the payroll—a belief underscored by the ability of Ander-son's clients to obtain favorable treatment in state agencies. In one example, Davis's health director sent a letter discouraging a private foundation from sin-gling out the Rite-Aid drugstore chain for criticism for selling cigarettes. The foundation had received a grant of state funds for its antismoking campaign and Rite-Aid was an Anderson client. By the end of Davis' first year in office, Anderson's grandiosely named firm, Platinum Advisors, was raking in a half-million dollars each quarter in retainers, and some old-line lobbyists were grum-bling that he was violating the lobbying corps' informal rules against one lobby-ist trying to lure away clients from another. Some senior lobbyists paid a per-sonal visit to Anderson and warned him about alienating others in the fraternity by raiding their client lists—which Anderson insisted he wasn't doing.

And then there are the "goo-goos," which is Capitol shorthand for "good government types," lobbyists who put in long hours and are paid ditch digger wages on behalf of causes, ranging from political reform to college fees to sav-ing the environment. The goo-goos, many of whom ensconce themselves in an aged office building three blocks from the Capitol, known as the "goo-goo ghetto," because of its proximity and cheap rents, form a distinct subculture in the Capitol. They operate just as their better-paid counterparts do, gathering information, cultivating contacts among legislators and Capitol staffers, and forming strategic alliances. But they lack the capacity to buy tickets to expensive fundraising events like the money players, and they seldom have the staff that government lobbyists employ, or the ability of government agencies to hire high-priced contract lobbyists and feed off the access they obtain by spending private clients' money on campaign contributions. The goo-goos live by their wits and, like so many guerrilla warriors, off the land, using media stunts, grassroots activism, and what they hope is the power of moral persuasion to affect the outcome of the issues that they lobby. Goo-goo interests—Common Cause, for one—are inveterate issuers of news releases, studies, and compilations of data, and their lobbyists make themselves easily available to reporters in hopes of attracting media attention to their causes.

One distinct trend of the past generation has been a strong flow of women into the lobbying corps, paralleling their incursions into other previously all-male fields. And that has given rise to suspicions among male lobbyists that their curvier colleagues may enjoy an advantage when dealing with a Legislature still composed mostly of men spending several days each week away from their families.

CHAPTER 3

The Field General of Political Warfare

War is the continuation of policy by other means (and) is the province of chance. In no other sphere of human activity must such a margin be left for this intruder. It increases the uncertainty of any circumstance and deranges the course of events—Karl von Clausewitz, in On War, *1833*

Jerry Brown's election as governor of California in 1975, energized activists of all ideological stripes—but particularly those on the left. After eight years of Ronald Reagan, reformers felt empowered by the 36-year-old Democratic governor whose political roots were in the civil rights and farm worker unionization movements as well as in his father's own activist governorship.

One of the many ways in which this new activism manifested itself was in a series of "sleep-ins" in the outer lobby of the governor's suite in the southeast corner of the Capitol building, a tactic borrowed from the college campus civil rights and anti-Vietnam War protests of the 1960s. Shouting slogans and toting leaflets, demonstrators for a wide variety of causes would occupy the governor's vestibule, hoping to garner media attention, particularly from the Los Angeles and San Francisco television stations that maintained bureaus at the Capitol and were always eager for pictures of people doing something to enliven the dry and colorless business of politics. And there was always a chance that Brown himself, a bachelor who kept odd hours and slept on a mattress on the floor of a sparsely furnished apartment across the street from the Capitol, would pay the demonstrators a visit.

One of those 1975 sleep-in demonstrations was especially noteworthy, since it was conducted by several dozen well-dressed, obviously affluent white women who brought down-filled sleeping bags and other creature comforts to their Capitol pajama party and who had their meals catered by one of Sacramento's tonier restaurants. Clearly, these were no farm workers or poverty protesters. They were, in fact, the wives of medical doctors who were doing their bit to dramatize one of the many issues that confronted the Legislature and the new governor that year: a crisis in medical malpractice insurance that, it was said, threatened the availability of quality care, particularly in obstetrics.

No one could have predicted at the time that the demonstration by the doctors' wives, which did attract widespread media attention, would be the beginning of a decades-long political war with stakes in the tens of billions of dollars, one that was still raging a quarter-century. The conflict, pitting medical care providers against personal injury attorneys, would become a case study in the ever-evolving dynamics of the Capitol and the techniques that lobbyists devise to persuade the Legislature and other political policy bodies to do what their clients want.

The analogy to war is not overstated, for a Capitol political conflict contains all of the elements of a military campaign with the exception—at least most of the time—of bloodshed, to wit:

- The lobbyist is, in effect, the field general who depends on his support organization, his clients, for resources and support as much as General Dwight Eisenhower depended on General George Marshall in Washington during World War II, or General Norman Schwarzkopf counted on Gen. Colin Powell to handle the home front during the Persian Gulf War. The lobbyist, like other field generals, must rely on his supporters for financial and material backing, and sometimes for warm bodies to flood the Capitol or make telephone calls, and knows that it's foolish to go into war without confidence that the support will be unwavering and instantly available.
- The lobbyist and his clients must have a clear understanding about what the situation is and what goals are to be accomplished, including fallback positions should their initial goals prove to be unrealistic or too costly. Knowing when to quit, either accepting a partial victory or a loss, is as important in political war as in the real thing, lest one overreach or look foolish and undercut the ability to fight again.
- The lobbyist/general, having developed a firm understanding with his clients on goals and resources, must devise a strategy he believes will lead to victory, whether it's the passage of legislation or adoption of administrative policy that enhances his clients' interests, or the defeat of efforts by rival interests to do the same, based on his evaluation of the Capitol battlefield, the assets of the enemy, and the capability of the rival or rivals to wage war.
- Finally, the plan must be implemented competently and flexibly, with the understanding that circumstances can change rapidly once the battle is

joined and that imagination, verve, and guts count just as much in the halls of the Capitol as they do in war. Some lobbyists, like some generals and admirals, demonstrate a knack for winning battle after battle while others just can't cut it. And until the shooting begins, it's difficult to say which it will be.

Where political war differs from the military variety, of course, is that the tactics are much different, and experienced lobbyists use one or more of 12 general approaches when gaming a situation in the Capitol, often using one process to influence outcomes of another in a calculated strategy to reach the desired result, to wit:

1.   **Win on the merits.** This is always the preferred course if it's available because it's the cheapest and cleanest. Appealing to the common sense of those who make the decision will often prevail in a minor matter when there is no organized opposition. If the client wants some simple change of law that will not cost anyone very much and can be defended on the grounds of good public policy—changing the way corporate tax returns are filed to make them simpler, for instance—it's usually just a matter of running it by the affected state agencies, if any, and the consultants to the policy committees in the Legislature, getting a legislator to introduce and carry the bill and arranging some testimony at committee hearings to make the case. Most of the thousands of bills introduced in every biennial session of the Legislature fall into this minor league, having little or no impact on any organized interest group. Minority party legislators eagerly solicit these innocuous measures from state agencies, local governments, and private interests because they are frozen out of carrying major legislation, particularly of the moneyed variety, by the majority party and have no other means of improving their legislative scorecards. It's often smart for a lobbyist to use a minority party legislator to carry such a bill because the lawmaker will give it much more attention than a majority party politician who has bigger and juicier fish to fry. If, however, the issue is a controversial one, with significant opposition, appeals to logic and merits have little to do with the outcome. That's when professional warriors are brought into the battle.

2.   **Win procedurally.** Outfox the opposition through cunning and a better understanding of legislative rules, customs, or protocols of the Capitol. Any legislation must survive a series of hurdles—committee and floor votes and a governor's signature—to make it into law. The process is essentially a negative one because a bill can clear seven of the eight major hurdles (plus other minor ones) and still lose if it bangs into the eighth one. If a lobbyist is trying to get a bill passed, a procedural approach seeks to bypass as many hurdles as possible to give the opposition fewer opportunities to shoot down the bill. Thus, for example, a lobbyist might take advantage of a section in legislative rules, often invoked in the Senate but less so in the Assembly, that allows a bill to bypass the appropriations committee of each house if it has little or no fiscal impact. If a bill is stalled in one committee by opposition lobbying, the advocate for the

measure can attach it, in the form of an amendment, to another bill that's further along in the process or use time-tested techniques, such as the conference committee or floor amendments, to skip perilous committee votes altogether. If, on the other hand, the goal is to kill a bill, one can enlist friendly lawmakers to raise objections to the procedural shortcuts taken by its proponents, forcing more committee or floor votes, offer up crippling amendments, or otherwise use the Legislature's arcane procedures to delay and buy time to employ other tactics. Procedural tactics can be effective, but they raise suspicions that one has a weak case on the bill's merits and if used too often can damage the lobbyist's reputation, thus undercutting his relationships with other lobbyists and legislators that are based on mutual trust.

The final days of any legislative session produce numerous attempts to "low ball" legislation, some of which has never been publicly aired in any legislative forum, as the lobbyists and legislators who specialize in such tactics do their thing, sometimes successfully and sometimes not.

The Wickland Oil incident cited in the previous chapter is just one of countless examples of the syndrome. Another, more recent, one is what happened in the last two days of the 1999 legislative session when a seemingly moribund Assembly bill was suddenly amended just 48 hours before the Legislature was due to adjourn for the year and jammed through both houses despite unanticipated media coverage and the efforts of lobbyists recruited at the last moment by the targeted interest groups. California grocery store chains and the retail clerks union, acting in concert with the Legislature's Democratic leaders, were behind the legislation that would effectively put "big box" retailers such as Wal-Mart and Costco out of the grocery business. It was a deliberate effort to jam the bill through the Capitol, virtually without public notice and hearings, that had been planned for months. But even though the measure moved onto Governor Gray Davis's desk with Democratic leaders marshaling the votes, the subsequent uproar in the media over the tactics and an effective organizational campaign to flood Davis's office with protests from the discount stores' customers spelled doom. Although the Capitol rumor mill had indicated that Davis would sign the bill at the behest of a major grocery store tycoon who was one of his closest personal friends and political allies—and the employer of his wife Sharon—the first-term governor vetoed it, citing the tactics used to gain its enactment.

It was the sort of thing that could only be tried once because the big discount retailers were on alert for a repeat in the following year, and city and county governments, whose sales tax revenues could have been imperiled by legislation making it more difficult for the big boxes to operate, made it clear that they would join any future battle. Indeed, the big boxers and local governments even threatened an initiative campaign to thwart their rivals with a constitutional amendment and/or a referendum to repeal any anti-big box law that might be enacted. And the media uproar over the issue created a backlash. Some Democrats who voted for the big box bill were hammered by Republican challengers in 2000 for taking part in what even the governor said was a sleazy attempt to circumvent the legislative process. While short-lived, the big box battle was almost a throwback to the older days of legislative gamesmanship—and resulted in fat fees for lobbyists thrown into the war at the last moment. One hired by the big box stores thanked a rival lobbyist for creating some unanticipated business and income.

3. Win through grassroots activation, which is becoming a more important technique with the advent of legislative term limits. The rapid turnover of legislators and Capitol staffers mandated by term limits prevents lobbyists from developing long-term, one-on-one relationships with decisionmakers, Term limits also bring into the Capitol more real people—business owners, teachers, farmers, local government officials, etc.—who have a continuing interest in and relationship with local news media, local civic and political leaders, and local organizations, such as chambers of commerce. In such an atmosphere, one-on-one lobbying, while still important, has faded and lobbying by local activists has become more potent. If, for example, one is lobbying on a matter affecting auto repair shops, it helps immensely if the legislator whose committee vote is pivotal on the issue gets a telephone call, or a personal visit, from a prominent garage owner in his home town to describe how the legislation affects him.

While professionally generated grassroots organization work can be costly it can also be very effective, as the doctors' wives demonstrated in the 1970s and the big box retailers' public relations and political strategists showed in 1999. It's one of the few tools that interest groups lacking the money for campaign contributions and big-name lobbyists can use to offset the monetary resources of their rivals. Environmentalists, consumer advocates, and others have proved that grassroots organization can be valuable adjuncts to their lobbyists' work inside the Capitol.

4. Win by mobilizing public opinion through "paid media." While paid media advertisements are common in political campaigns, both for and against candidates and ballot measures, their use in legislative issue battles is rarer because it's very expensive—several million dollars for a decent statewide campaign—and a crapshoot in terms of effectiveness. One example is what happened in 1999, during the first year of Gray Davis's governorship, when he was faced with a decision on whether to immediately ban use of the controversial gasoline additive MTBE, as health advocates and environmentalists were demanding (even though its use was mandated in the first place to clean up the air). MTBE makers, seeking a phase out over several years to amortize their investment in equipment, placed a series of newspaper ads warning, that an immediate ban on the compound would increase smog and laying the issue directly on Davis. The governor, who dislikes confrontations of any kind, was livid about being singled out in the ads but he did what the companies wanted, ordering a multi-year phaseout. Would he have done it anyway or did the ads tip the balance? Only Davis knows for certain.

5. Win by mobilizing public opinion through influencing the news media, both in terms of news coverage and editorial opinion. This form of political warfare has emerged only in the last couple of decades, along with a new breed of political warrior: the media consultant. These operatives, termed "flacks" by reporters, are often former reporters themselves, or they may be college-trained public relations specialists. Their function, as part of the overall strategy, is to use their media connections to encourage reporters to cover certain stories, supply information on behalf of their clients, meet with newspaper editorial boards, and ghost-write "op-ed" articles on behalf of their clients. One example of many is the late 1980s drive to crack down on sales of tobacco products to minors, which was aided immeasurably by a media campaign mounted by the California Medical Association through a media consulting firm. Media specialists proliferated in the Capitol during the 1990s, thanks to the increasing sophistication of interest groups about the role of the media in setting the political agenda and the arrival of term limits, which brought to the Capitol many neophyte legislators who were more sensitive to the media than their professional predecessors. The media consultants are, in fact, lobbyists of the media, and there have been proposals that they register as lobbyists themselves.

6. Win with a silver bullet—a single shot that takes out the target with no collateral damage. It's a technique that is almost always used to defeat a bill and almost never to pass one. And it works only if the lobbyist and/or his public relations adviser have found something in the bill that, if it became public knowledge, would be too damaging for the measure to survive. There are a few—very few—PR consultants working the Capitol who specialize in this technique because there are only a few of them smart and devious enough to make it work. They conduct deep opposition research, ferret out the motives of the other side, delve into the legislation for stuff that would naturally interest a journalist, and deliver the damaging material to someone in the Capitol press corps with whom they have a mutually trusting relationship. The reporter gets his exclusive, legitimately newsworthy story and the PR agent gets his information published without going through the hoops of a press conference, which is rarely as effective because its bias is evident. One practitioner of the technique not only deals with newspaper reporters in Sacramento, trying to interest them in writing about particular bills with demonstrable success, but plows even more difficult, if inherently richer, ground by generating stories for television stations in Los Angeles and San Francisco, which don't maintain bureaus in the Capitol. A former television field producer, he will go so far as to hire his own videotape crew, shoot the story just as if he were a working journalist and deliver a finished product to television stations that's so credible and professionally done that many news directors will simply air it as is, without further editing. He'll even produce different versions of the same story for different stations in the same market.

The resulting stories may not portray the political marksman's own employers in the best light—their motives in killing the bill may be just as self-serving as those of the proponents—but that's not important. What is important is that the measure be portrayed, accurately, as a crass, pocket-lining maneuver, thus making legislators very reluctant to vote for it. Bills caught with their pants down, as it were, are often scuttled with no further action. A subtle version of the technique is to offer the embarrassing story to a local newspaper or television station in the district of the legislator carrying the bill or the lawmaker who's the pivotal committee vote on the bill—a story that may never surface in Sacramento but embarrasses the targeted politician enough that he distances himself from the issue. If used, this technique must be done completely without fingerprints because nothing will alienate a legislator more than learning that a lobbyist or someone allied with him has besmirched him in his own district. When two political secret agents find themselves on opposite sides of the issue at hand, the action comes to resemble something out of *Mad* magazine's old "Spy vs. Spy" comic strip.

One example illustrates how deadly a silver bullet can be. In the late 1970s, during one of California's periodic gasoline supply/price crises—a matter of great interest in a state with 25 million registered vehicles consuming a billion gallons of gasoline a month—a southern California assemblyman named Terry Goggin garnered much media attention with legislation that would, he said, compel oil companies to divest themselves of their service stations and thereby introduce more competition into the fuel trade. One day, as the debate over the bill raged, a major oil company lobbyist happened to encounter a newspaper reporter on a street corner near the Capitol and as the two chatted and exchanged gossip, the lobbyist asked the reporter whether he was familiar with the Goggin bill. The reporter replied that he knew about it, but had written nothing about it yet. The lobbyist reached into his jacket pocket, pulled out a copy of the bill and showed the reporter a very obscure section that said the service station divestiture mandate would not apply to any oil company meeting specific criteria. "Did you know that this would exempt just one company?" the lobbyist asked the reporter, anticipating and receiving a negative reply. "It's Douglas Oil," the lobbyist continued, referring to what was then one of southern California's major "independent" refiners and service station operators. "And do you know who's father was executive vice president of Douglas Oil?" the lobbyist asked. By then, the reporter had an idea where this was leading. "Is it Goggin?" the reporter responded. "Yes," the lobbyist confirmed. The reporter's story about Goggin exempting his father's company, one in which his family had extensive holdings, appeared the next morning and within hours, Goggin had dropped the bill, a victim of the silver bullet, albeit one that Goggin himself had loaded into the sniper's rifle. The encounter between the lobbyist and the reporter was not planned by either party; the two were acquaintances who just happened to run into each other on the street and exchange gossip and chatter. But the result was just as effective as if an entire platoon of lobbyists had been dispatched, an extensive advertising campaign had been conducted and thousands of dollars in campaign checks had been written. A few years later, Goggin was defeated in the Democratic primary as he sought re-election. Local newspapers had laid out a series of instances in which his legislation had become intertwined with his personal finances.

7. Win by burying the issue in the state budget or one of the many "budget trailer bills" that are hastily assembled and even more hastily enacted, supposedly to implement the annual budget bill. These companion measures are a fairly recent phenomenon, but the fact that they are given very little scrutiny before enactment makes them perfect vehicles for doing things that, in truth, have little or nothing to do with the budget. The goal may be accomplished with an appropriation buried among many, or by language dictating how certain funds can and cannot be spent. The Legislature has posted guards that supposedly spot and highlight efforts to use the budget or its companion measures as vehicles, but the safeguards have become increasingly easy to bypass.

8. Win at the ballot box. The initiative and the referendum were enacted nearly a century ago as reforms to break the stranglehold on special interests on the state Capitol. If the people could make laws directly through the initiative or overturn laws enacted by the Legislature through the referendum, early 20th-century reformers such as Hiram Johnson contended, lawmakers would be more circumspect. In fact, neither of these techniques—both of which involve collecting names of registered voters on petitions to win a place on the ballot—was used very much for more than a half century after their enactment. Whitaker and Baxter, a pioneer San Francisco public relations/political consulting firm, first demonstrated how special interests could use the ballot box to trump the Legislature but it fell to a pair of crusty political gadflies named Howard Jarvis and Paul Gann to drive home the potential of the initiative to exploit popular sentiment. The two teamed up to place Proposition 13, California's historic property tax limitation measure, on the 1978 primary election ballot. Their demonstration of the initiative petition's power coincided with a rising level of popular frustration at the seeming lethargy of the Legislature and the evolution of more sophisticated direct mail fundraising and petition circulation techniques that made the qualification of ballot measures more feasible.

In the two decades that followed, dozens of measures made their way onto Californians' ballots. Some of them were true grassroots efforts, such as Mike Reynolds' three-strikes-and-you're-out law. Some were generated by politicians themselves as publicity vehicles to assist some larger goal, such as Governor Pete Wilson's 1994 measure limiting public benefits to illegal immigrants that helped him win re-election. And some were purely special interest battles stemming from frustration with stalemate in the Legislature. The latter category includes five measures related to auto insurance that crowded the 1988 ballot and generated upwards of $100 million in campaign spending, a record until Indian tribes and Nevada gambling interests spent even more a decade later in battling over two measures legalizing their gambling operations (the first Indian casino measure was invalidated by the courts after lawsuits were filed by rival gambling interests). The Indian gambling measures were also stark examples of how the ballot can be used to simply undo what the politicians have wrought in the Capitol. The casino-owning tribes placed the first measure on the ballot to dismantle the restrictions that a hostile governor, Pete Wilson, had imposed on gambling while the second was to ratify what a very friendly governor, Gray Davis, agreed to implement just months later.

Sometimes the threat of an initiative will break a stalemate or achieve a compromise. When, for instance, advocates of charter schools were frustrated by lobbyists for the California Teachers Association in their drive to expand the number of the quasi-independent schools, they threatened to go to the voters with an even more expansive measure. The threat was credible because the charter school backers included some Silicon Valley tycoons who had taken a personal interest in educational reform and it led to a compromise expanding the number of charter schools. A few years later, the California Teachers Association itself used the same technique, threatening to place on the ballot an initiative that would have required California to raise per-pupil school spending to the national average. On the very day it would have turned in its petitions, the CTA made a school financing deal with Governor Gray Davis, who was bitterly opposed to having the measure appear on the ballot.

The referendum, challenging a law already enacted, has been even more rarely invoked. But one example of how it could turn a high-stakes political battle arose in 2000, when major auto insurance companies pledged $50 million for a referendum drive to overturn a new law that subjected them to "bad faith" lawsuits. The law, a high-priority goal of personal injury attorneys, was rejected by voters after lawyers were unable to muster more than a token amount of campaign money to defend it—a skirmish in the never-ending struggle over tort law that's waged on many fronts. Beyond its direct impact, the successful referendum campaign demonstrated that it can be an effective weapon and therefore a credible threat to use it has become a new weapon to be deployed during showdowns under the Capitol dome.

   9.   **Win by negotiations.** Often, competing interest groups find themselves in a stalemate, neither able to move and neither wanting to accept the status quo because each would have to maintain a constant state of alert against some maneuver by the other—the trench warfare of World War I being the military analogy. That's when negotiations, either directly or through intermediaries, can either result in a mutually acceptable compromise or at least a truce. There is, in every serious conflict between competing interest groups, what lobbyists call the "magic moment" when a compromise is within reach and each faction must decide to seize the moment or carry the fight into another time and perhaps another arena. Perhaps the most famous—or infamous, depending on one's view of the

outcome—example of a negotiated settlement in recent Capitol history was the "napkin deal" worked out in Frank Fat's restaurant late one night in 1987 over the rules governing personal injury lawsuits. Over the course of a months-long legislative session, hundreds of less sensational deals are worked out among lobbyists on issues large and small. For the most part, legislators love them because they are relieved of the onus of taking sides, being inherently less interested in what is being done than in their roles in the process itself.

10. Win by moving the issue into the courts, which at the very least can buy time to allow the purely political techniques to have an effect. When, for example, the California Medical Association's physician members complained about being increasingly restricted by managed health care companies (HMOs) in what services they could perform for their patients, the medical lobby found itself unable to resolve the conflict in the Legislature due to the political clout of HMOs, born of their lavish campaign contributions. The CMA then filed a lawsuit, scoring several significant wins and bringing pressure to bear on the HMOs and the Legislature to address the issue—pressure that was enhanced by the declining public image of HMOs due to adverse media exposure and even barbs in movies and television shows. Short of an actual lawsuit, an interest group can use the legal system to its advantage through such techniques as obtaining favorable opinions from the attorney general's office that put a rival interest on the defensive.

11. Win by postlegislative administrative action. Legislatures may decree but the job of implementing any piece of legislation is usually left to the administrative agencies, often—but not always—under the control of the governor. The real-world impact of any legislative act may be determined by a directive from the governor's office, the formulation of administrative regulations, or a decision by some board or commission, and a loss in the legislative arena can often be negated by continuing the battle in the administrative one. It's not unknown for a governor to sign a bill proclaiming that some wonderful result will occur and then undercut the legislation with administrative actions once the television cameras have vanished. Often, lobbyists find themselves operating purely in the administrative realm on issues that have nothing to do with legislation, although sometimes enlisting legislators in their drives. That's particularly true when the goal is obtaining a state agency contract or a favorable ruling from some agency on a pending policy matter. However, when an administrative action adversely affects a client, a lobbyist can pursue a reversal through legislation.

12. Win the old-fashioned way by buying it. It's illegal to bribe a legislator with either campaign funds or some form of personal income, as several former inmates of federal prison could attest. But short of an actual *quid pro quo* arrangement in which votes are traded for money, there's little doubt that campaign money plays a major role in deciding who wins and who loses in Capitol clashes, particularly those seen by Capitol insiders as grabs for market share or some competitive advantage. The prevailing opinion is that since some interest is profiting handsomely from the measure at hand, legislators' campaign treasuries should get a share—usually a small share—of the booty. The trick to effective use of campaign checks is to issue them in such a way that overt bribery is avoided, but the legislator who receives the contribution knows that it's conditioned on his continued friendliness to the contributor.

The truly effective "political action" campaigns in the Capitol to pass or defeat legislation never rely on just one of these twelve techniques. Although any one of them can, under the right circumstances, turn the trick, one never knows in advance which will be the most effective, just as a military general wants to have different kinds of forces at his command to use singly or in conjunction with one another to exploit whatever opportunity the battlefield presents. Sometimes he needs tanks, sometimes he needs infantry, sometimes he needs artillery, and sometimes he needs air strikes, so he always needs to have all of his forces in battle-ready condition.

The lobbyist who's commanding one side of a political war also wants to use the minimal amount of resources—campaign money, lobbying time, public relations work, etc.—necessary to reach the end goal of passing or killing the legislation at hand, no matter how much firepower he may have in reserve, just as a military commander wants to be judicious in commitment of forces to avoid depleting his reserves. Unless there's a clear reason to do otherwise, a lobbyist wants to begin his campaign at the least intensive level—arguing his case on its merits—and escalate into other techniques only as needed. It's one of the basic axioms of the trade because the deployment of every new weapon makes a negotiated settlement more difficult and risks a backlash of resentment from those who get caught in the crossfire, as well as opposition interests and lobbyists with whom the lobbyist might form an alliance on some future issue. And overkill could even backfire on the current issue if others in the arena decide that the overreaching lobbyist needs to be taught a lesson in good manners. It's happened more than once in the Capitol, although it's doubtful than any lobbyist has ever admitted it when telling a client that the battle has been lost.

It goes without saying that every win, by whatever strategy, implies a loss by some other interest group—except, of course, for the negotiated settlement. Therefore—again as in any military campaign—the lobbyist must see to his or her defenses as well as plot the offensive strategy. If, for example, one is trying to pass a bill and senses that the opposition is about to unleash a media barrage of some kind, it might make sense to make a preemptive strike that will blunt the effect of the opposition assault, and perhaps head it off altogether. Or if a lobbyist senses that one of his key committee votes is wavering and beginning to veer to the other side, it may be time to call in the shock troops—perhaps a timely visit or a phone call from some influential folks from his district, what some call "significant constituents."

Often, no matter how diligently a lobbyist practices tradecraft, the skirmish will be lost, and that's when he or she must face the client—and perhaps the music. The postsession autumnal conferences with clients are among the toughest periods in any lobbyist's year, especially contract lobbyists who must renegotiate their agreements. "That's when we do some our best lobbying," says one veteran of Capitol wars. Does the defeated lobbyist admit to shortcomings, does he inferentially blame the client for a lack of support, or does he lay defeat at the door of a richer opponent? The old adage about victory having many fathers and defeat being an orphan is very applicable to these postmortem sessions. One contract lobbyist for city governments who shall go unnamed sent a series of dispatches to a municipal client explaining why he could not obtain a relatively small appropriation for a city park in 2000, a year in which the state had more than $12 billion in budget surpluses. The lobbyist told city officials that they lost out because they had too many white residents. "In short, those cities not representing minority citizens and not being represented by minority representatives did not receive funding," said one summary of the lobbyist's explanation. City officials were incensed at this apparent discrimination, and the memos were leaked to a reporter. But when the journalist confronted the lobbyist about the situation, the advocate—clearly shocked that his private communications were becoming public—sheepishly admitted to the reporter that he had concocted the explanation to cover his posterior with his client.

Fudging to the client on what happened and why is just one of the unethical games that are part of the lobbying trade, despite efforts to bring professionalism and codes of conduct to the field. Others include stringing out an issue, sometimes for years, to maximize lobbying fees (a years-long battle over taxation of multinational corporations is considered one example); fabricating obstacles to persuade a gullible client that the task at hand is more difficult, and thus more expensive, than previously thought; sacrificing a client's interests to cultivate relations with legislators who can help with other, more lucrative employers; selling more than 100 percent of the available time, which means someone isn't getting a first-class effort; putting more effort into selling the client on the contract than delivering the goods; running up costs after submitting low-ball bids for lobbying business; and stealing clients, often by bad-mouthing the potential client's current representation, a technique sometimes used by individual lobbyists to peel away business from a large, multi-interest organization.

The war over medical malpractice and other, closely related personal injury lawsuit issues eventually involved an entire arsenal of offensive and defensive political weaponry that's still being deployed as the new century begins, as well as an entire generation of political warriors. One lobbyist working the issue in 2000 was in grade school when it first erupted in 1975 with doctors, especially obstetricians and anesthesiologists, being hit with huge increases in their medical malpractice insurance premiums, thanks to a spate of lawsuits and a sharp escalation in the awards that juries were making to patients claiming injuries from poor medical practices.

The origins of the premium increases are still being debated because the malpractice conflict itself is still alive in the Capitol. Doctors believe that greedy personal injury attorneys began filing the suits in large numbers as they sensed that juries were increasingly willing to make large awards of damages in malpractice cases, regardless of their true medical merits. Lawyers insist they are merely representing clients injured by an increasingly impersonal, uncaring, and profit-oriented medical system. Medical providers and their insurers reckoned their additional losses at a billion dollars a year, a substantial share of which—perhaps a third—was going to the lawyers as contingency fees.

It's part of a much-larger debate over the entire civil justice system, both in California and national circles—whether it's truly a forum in which plaintiffs and defendants can seek equitable treatment or a lottery in which attorneys seek out plaintiffs and file suits in hopes of hitting the jackpot on enough occasions to make the contingency fee system profitable, either through jury awards or settlements from insurers worried about what juries might do. Lawyers and their allies, mostly consumer activists in the Ralph Nader mold, and insurers and their compatriots, usually business and professional groups that are the targets of lawsuits, have battled in the Capitol and in the initiative arena over a wide variety of specific issues, not only malpractice but whether "deep pocket" defendants with little connection to the main case should bear inordinate burdens of paying damages, whether insurers should be susceptible to suits for bad faith handling of claims, whether corporations should be protected from "strike suits" alleging corporate malfeasance filed by attorneys when stock prices fall, and whether the tort system should be bypassed altogether by such devices as binding arbitration of disputes and/or no-fault coverage of motorists. Although other interest groups and other issues have risen and fallen in the consciousness of the Capitol over the years, no conflict has displayed the immense stakes and sheer longevity of the tort wars, occupying an entire generation of professional political soldiers.

The Capitol itself was in the throes of cultural change when the malpractice insurance crisis erupted in 1975. Not only did the state have a newly elected governor in Jerry Brown, but the 1974 elections—the first after a court-ordered reapportionment plan changed every legislative district in the state—had produced a bumper crop of new faces in the Capitol, marking a generational change from the quasi-amateurs who dominated the Legislature in the 1950s and 1960s to cool, process-oriented professionals, many of them veterans of the legislative staff itself. And Democrats having recaptured the governorship after eight years of Ronald Reagan, won all but one of the other statewide offices, and enhanced their majorities in both houses of the Legislature. The Assembly had a new speaker in Leo McCarthy, a veteran of San Francisco politics who, in an upset that surprised almost everyone, had bested Willie Brown to capture the powerful position.

Organized labor, environmentalists, consumer activists, and many other groups were papering the Capitol with what they deemed to be "progressive" legislation, hoping that liberal Democrats would enact much of their agenda into law—hopes that often became reality during the first years of the Brown governorship. Seemingly, therefore, it was an inhospitable climate for the enactment of a bill to impose limits on the awards that juries could make in medical malpractice cases—the sort of thing that conservative Republicans might champion. But the California Medical Association (CMA), spearheading the drive for malpractice damage limits, had conducted a massive grassroots organizational drive, had amassed a $4 million political warchest—huge by 1975 standards—and had drummed their message through the media that the premium increases would drive doctors out of the profession or out of the state and thus make it more difficult for California families to obtain care, especially obstetrical care. They also benefited from what was then a very high regard for the medical profession in the larger public, based on millions of individual relationships between physicians and patients, this being an era before "managed care" changed the medical culture and drove a wedge between patients and their doctors. Finally, even though they later became a fearsome Capitol power, the "trial lawyers" who filed and pressed personal injury lawsuits were poorly organized in 1975, often squabbling among themselves over political ends and means—a condition that still plagues the interest group to some degree.

Medical providers, especially doctors, laid out their public case, worked individual legislators through professional CMA lobbyists and with doctors themselves, capitalized on their position as one of the state's major sources of campaign funds, and implied that should they lose in the Legislature, they'd spend millions on an initiative drive that would enact an even stricter limit on personal injury judgments. Even so, their success in enacting the Medical Injury Compensation Reform Act (MICRA) was astonishing. The measure's four main provisions were a limit on lawyers' contingency fees, elimination of multiple payments from multiple sources, allowing malpractice awards to be paid in installments rather than in lump sums and, most importantly, a $250,000 cap on the noneconomic ("pain and suffering") damages that had been the vehicle for the sharp increase in jury judgments. And the political victory was underscored when a liberal state Supreme Court, by a 4–3 vote, upheld the measure's provisions despite the lawyers' firm belief that they could prevail at that level no matter what happened in the Legislature.

MICRA worked marvelously, as far as the medical providers were concerned. Three years after its enactment, the number of lawyers handling medical malpractice cases in California dropped from 2,000 to 200, the number of so-called "jumbo" malpractice judgments declined by 80 percent, and malpractice insurance premiums stabilized. National medical organizations took notice and began beating the drums for similar changes in other states and even in Congress.

It was a huge loss for the lawyers, a group that does not relish losing in any arena, and a wakeup call about their poor position in the Capitol. They began worrying not only about MICRA being taken to other states, but the extension of MICRA-like limits to other personal injury cases, such as auto crashes, product liability, and environmental damages. The California Trial Lawyers Association (later to become Consumer Attorneys of California) went into political prize-fight training, firing its Sacramento lobbyist, reorganizing its support staff and grassroots and media operations, and, most of all, beginning to raise millions of dollars to donate to campaigns and reestablish its position in the Capitol. Large litigation firms imposed assessments on themselves to build the CTLA's political treasury and the organization's staff was given additional authority to wheel and deal. Initially, the lawyers harbored hopes of winning a quick repeal or major modification of the new law, but with the election of Republican George Deukmejian as Jerry Brown's successor in 1982 and eight years later the continuation of Republican control of the governor's office with Pete Wilson, the lawyers' hopes were stymied.

The attorneys suffered another major setback when voters approved a business-backed initiative to restrict "deep pocket" awards but were able to turn back insurance company-sponsored measures that would have created a "no fault" auto insurance system. By the late 1980s, the tort wars had become a fixture of Capitol life, each side taking turns either in the Legislature or in the initiative arena at gaining ground on the other. And the conflict came to a head with the decision of a business coalition to pursue an initiative that would extend MICRA's provisions to other lawsuits, a measure called PICRA for the Personal Injury Compensation Reform Act, and a counter threat by lawyers to write their own pro lawsuit initiative that would hit corporations and insurers hard. For months in early 1987, the contending factions raised money, beefed up their grassroots organizations, retained political consultants and initiative signature-gathering firms, conducted polls, had bills introduced in the Legislature, threatened crippling lawsuits and in many other ways prepared for serious political war—or at least pretended to do so to rattle the rival groups.

Tort warriors on both sides were faced with either continuing the battle, and its PICRA escalation, or seeking a kind of compromise and/or truce. After months of saber-rattling, feints, shouting matches, and abortive private talks, it came down to that fateful night at Frank Fat's restaurant, an art deco bistro three blocks from the Capitol that for decades had been the watering hole and feeding site of choice for the Capitol's most influential figures, as well as the venue for high-stakes poker games. The business coalition's lobbyists, some of the most experienced in the trade, had agreed among themselves that PICRA would go on the ballot unless every segment of the group got something of value from the negotiations, nobody would be split away by making a separate deal with the lawyers, and no coalition member would be asked to give up something without getting something in return. Although negotiations had been underway, fitfully, for weeks prior to that final night, the 1987 legislative session was drawing to a close, as was the practical deadline for beginning the gathering of signatures for the PICRA initiative. Pointedly, the business coalition's signature-gatherers set up tables around the Capitol to demonstrate that the moment of truth was near. Negotiators, who included some key legislators, set a 6 p.m. deadline for agreement or collapse and as the hour neared, both sides gave ground and a settlement appeared possible. They agreed to extend the deadline to 11 p.m. and break for dinner, adjourning to nearby Frank Fat's with the factions sitting at separate tables but continuing to talk through emissaries—often legislators—and offering toasts to each other's sagacity. By 9 p.m., most of the contested issues had been resolved but there were a few sticky points that could scuttle the incipient deal, and prospects were actually dimming when Willie Brown, Speaker of the Assembly (he succeeded Leo McCarthy in 1980 after a bitter, year-long battle between McCarthy and another rival), swaggered through the front door of Fat's with his characteristic panache.

Brown worked the room in his usual flamboyant style, stopping at the bar to chat with power brokers and lawmakers, hugging the attractive women, exchanging jokes and jibes and, finally, offering to become a mediator for the tort warriors. It was a situation that Brown simply loved, being able to bring his raging intellect, encyclopedic knowledge, and persuasive ways to bear on a political situation and become the catalyst for the deal. Throughout his career, Brown was more interested in making the deal than its actual contents, whatever the issue. Methodically, he broke down the issue to its essential components and shuttling from faction to faction, knocked heads and cajoled reluctant participants, finally achieving settlement on all but one issue: whether the contingency fees in medical malpractice cases, limited by MICRA 12 years earlier to certain percentages, should be allowed to rise. Brown walked over to the health care coalition's chief lobbyist and told him he had been informed that the medical community's bottom line was more flexible than the lobbyist had insisted. The lobbyist looked the speaker in the eye and told him that "Your informant is wrong" and offered to call the president of the California Medical Association on the spot to confirm the CMA's position, an offer that Brown accepted. The CMA president told Brown that the lobbyist had full authority. And with a few tweaks, the CMA's adamant position on a relatively small increase in contingency fees was written into the agreement.

The outline of the deal was jotted down on a Frank Fat's tablecloth and within hours, the precise drafting of the complex agreement had begun. Its provisions included not only the slightly increased contingency fees in malpractice cases, but a suspension of the PICRA campaign, a tightening of the rules of proof governing punitive damages in personal injury cases, substantial immunity from lawsuits for makers of "inherently dangerous" products such as cigarettes (tobacco companies had a lobbyist at the table), and a five-year truce in which all tort warriors agreed not to back any legislation or initiative substantially changing the rules of personal injury suits—with a collateral pledge by the legislative leadership to enforce the truce by killing any bills that violated it.

State Senator Bill Lockyer, one of the legislators who had orbited on the periphery of the Frank Fat's negotiations, copied the outline onto a napkin and the next day proudly held it up for all to see in the Senate chambers, even as the deal's provisions were hustled into law before any outside reaction could scuttle it. The napkin was later featured on a poster, signed by the participants in the historic negotiations, that still is displayed in the entryway of Frank Fat's. Years later, the deal came to haunt both Lockyer and Brown when smoking and the tobacco industry became political pariahs. Both were slammed by opponents for protecting the tobacco industry from lawsuits as they ran for new positions, Brown the San Francisco mayor's office and Lockyer the attorney generalship, although both won. Lockyer insisted that he had been unaware that tobacco companies were benefited by the deal, an assertion that struck other participants as ludicrous. And the protection was later repealed by the Legislature.

The napkin deal was, of course, the antithesis of the textbook democracy that Capitol tour guides instill in school children as they troop through the building by the thousands each spring. It was an important change in personal injury law with multimillion, even multibillion, dollar consequences, hammered out in private by special interest advocates and then hustled into law with virtually no public notice or participation. And for years thereafter political reformers would cite it as an example of what's wrong with Sacramento, even as the lobbyist community celebrated it as the epitome of what lobbying in Sacramento is about.

But for the specific lobbyists involved in the napkin deal and their clients, it was a win-win situation that protected their pocketbooks and produced a breather in the tort wars. The lawyers and their rivals were spared having to spend millions of dollars on a PICRA battle at the polls, the lawyers were protected from PICRA's probable enactment, which would have cost them untold millions of dollars in contingency fees, businesses and their insurers gained some protection against unpredictable punitive damages (some have estimated the savings at $1 billion a year), MICRA was protected for five years (worth perhaps $500 million a year to medical providers and insurers), trial lawyers gained about $100 million a year in additional contingency fees from loosening MICRA's limits, doctors and other medical providers were protected from punitive damages that insurance doesn't cover, insurance losses were made more predictable and—for better or worse—tobacco companies were protected for many years from the lawsuits that plagued them in other states.

When the truce expired in 1992, there was no immediate flood of legislation to undo what had been wrought at Frank Fat's. Democratic control of the Legislature effectively blocked any effort by business and insurance lobbyists to enact additional "tort reforms" while the Republican hold on the governorship kept trial lawyers at bay. Each side would make occasional stabs at breaking the stalemate with bills carried by friendly legislators, but both knew that the partisan split in the Capitol precluded any real action and the offensives were largely to probe each other's defenses, try out themes and tactics, and persuade their own rank-and-file members that the Sacramento lobbyists were still on the job. All of the factions used the five-year truce period and the lull that followed to improve their political warmaking capacity. Medical providers set up a specialized organization, Californians Allied for Patient Protection (CAPP), to conduct grassroots organizing, political fundraising, and lobbying toward the day when the battle would be joined again, and other business and professional groups revitalized the Association of Californians for Tort Reform (later the California Civil Justice Association) to do much the same. Lawyers changed the name of their organization, firmed up their strategic alliances with consumer activist groups, particularly those identified with Ralph Nader, and expanded their campaign contributions to Democrats, looking forward to the day when a Democrat would occupy the governor's office and be willing to sign legislation expanding the right to sue for personal injuries and collect damages.

That day came, or so the lawyers believed, in January 1999, when Gray Davis—who had been Jerry Brown's chief of staff when MICRA was enacted in 1975—was inaugurated as governor. Within days of Davis's investiture, the Consumer Attorneys of California—who preferred the acronym CAOC but whose detractors liked CACA for obvious reasons—had their allies introduce bills to repeal the MICRA pain and suffering cap, establish a new right to sue health maintenance organizations for their medical care decisions, and subject insurers to suits by third parties for bad faith handling of claims against policyholders. The latter issue stemmed from two state Supreme Court decisions, the first issued in 1979 by the liberal Rose Bird court that extended a long-standing right of policyholders to sue their own insurers to others making claims. Thus, for example, State Farm could be sued by a motorist who had been involved in an accident with a State Farm-covered driver, if State Farm didn't settle the claim to the satisfaction of the first motorist. The second decision 12 years later by a much more conservative court headed by Malcolm Lucas effectively repealed the first decision.

As trial lawyers and consumer advocates portrayed it, the ability of injured parties to sue insurers was needed to prevent the companies from stonewalling, lowballing settlement offers, and otherwise refusing to make reasonable settlements of claims against their clients. But insurers, citing data about the rise of third-party suits after the initial Bird court decision and their decline after the Lucas court repeal, said that the prospect of such bad faith suits, which could cost them untold millions of dollars in damages, was forcing them to make unreasonable settlements in the underlying injury cases. It was, as the insurers saw it, a tool of extortion. And to those in the Capitol, it was a huge money issue known as "Royal Globe" for the name of the original case.

During the 1980s, after the Bird court's first decision, insurance company lobbyists annually attempted to undo the Royal Globe ruling through legislation. But trial lawyers, having beefed up their lobbying and other political action capability after suffering an embarrassing setback on malpractice in 1975, turned back the insurers' legislative campaign through their influence with the Legislature's dominant Democrats. Trial lawyers have consistently contributed several million dollars to Democratic legislative campaign funds each two-year election cycle. The stakes for both sides in the battle, however, were many times larger—several billion dollars a year in additional insurance company payouts at least—and the Royal Globe conflict was unaffected by the 1987 napkin deal. But the tables were turned by the second Supreme Court decision in 1991, leading to a nine-year-long effort by the lawyers to reverse the situation again and reinstate the 1979 Rose Bird decision, a drive the trial attorneys' lobbyists hoped would bear fruit in 1999 after Davis became governor.

What the trial lawyers had hoped would be a big political—and financial—payoff on their three big issues in 1999, crumbled into dust for reasons that Capitol insiders are still pondering, but appear to be a mixture of changing political culture, some very sharp spadework and innovative tactics by their opponents, and a surprising lack of sophistication and focus by the attorneys.

One major reason for the lawyers' disappointment was that Davis turned out to be a Democrat who disliked controversy, especially anything that squeezed him between two powerful interest groups, and wanted to cultivate a friendly relationship with the business community. Although he had pledged to the trial lawyers before his election that he would sign a bad faith bill, he didn't specify what it would entail. He had never agreed during pre-election meetings to substantially change MICRA and although he had talked about HMO reform in his campaign, he hadn't specifically agreed to subject the health care companies to lawsuits.

There had been a cultural evolution, too, in the Legislature in the 12 years since the napkin deal. Voter approval of term limits in 1990 more or less deprofessionalized the Legislature. Fewer ex-legislative staffers ran for the Legislature, and more of its members were people who had pursued other professions, and/or local government and civic activities, before moving into the Legislature for relatively brief careers as lawmakers. They were, in other words, real people. Term limits, too, had severely weakened the once-total control that legislative leaders, such as the Assembly speaker, had wielded over the fate of legislation, which meant that no special interest group, including the seemingly powerful trial attorneys, could simply make a deal with the top leader and expect that it would be implemented—as, for instance, the podiatrists' lobby had done with Willie Brown in 1982.

The attorneys' lobbyists got a dose of that new reality when Cruz Bustamante, one of the post-Brown short-term speakers, tried to move a bill changing MICRA's limits on pain and suffering damages in his own house. Bustamante pleaded with his fellow Democrats to approve the bill and discharge his obligation to the trial lawyers, born of their lavish contributions to Democrats' campaign treasury that had helped end a brief Republican control of the house. "I owe these guys," Bustamante reportedly told Democrats during one private meeting. But his pleas were rejected as the Democratic caucus turned him down.

Not only were the lawyers still operating in the old mode of working through legislative leaders, but their opponents had adjusted to the new paradigm wrought by term limits. The California Medical Association, once a virtual adjunct of the state Republican party, had become a much more bipartisan entity and medical providers, through their CAPP organization dedicated to protecting MICRA, had spent years creating an effective grassroots network that would come into play.

Although their efforts through Bustamante had failed, the lawyers tried again with his successor as speaker, Antonio Villaraigosa, in 1999, hoping that with Davis in office, conditions might have improved for changing tort law. Villaraigosa fared only slightly better, winning from his Democratic caucus only permission to seek a cost of living increase in the $250,000 MICRA cap. And although Villaraigosa's bill passed the Assembly, trial lawyer lobbyists abandoned it in the Senate, seeing it as a small token that, if enacted, would block them from seeking a major increase or a repeal in the future.

The lawyers were losing, too, in their drive to subject the HMOs to lawsuits, despite the evident unpopularity of the health care companies with consumers—a situation that trial lawyers and their allies in the medical consumer groups had magnified with their own media campaign. The HMOs, realizing they had a big public relations and political problem in the Capitol, hired a new chief lobbyist who, ironically enough, had once headed the Common Cause political reform organization in California. The new lobbyist, Walter Zelman, had also done a stint in the Bill Clinton White House as a top aide in the administration's disastrous drive for a national health care program, and knew the subject inside and out. Zelman presented a friendlier face of the HMO industry, insisting that the health companies would agree to a set of reasonable reforms, including oversight by a new state agency and a dispute arbitration system he said would negate the need for lawsuits. The HMOs liberally distributed campaign funds, including a substantial chunk to the new governor, and when the dust had settled, Davis had obtained just what he wanted, a mild set of HMO reforms that theoretically allowed HMOs to be sued for their treatment decisions but severely undercut that right by allowing the HMOs to require their members to use binding arbitration to settle disputes as a condition of receiving coverage in the first place. The lawyers fumed but to no avail.

Only on the bad faith lawsuits, the one subject on which they had a pledge from Davis, did the lawyers make headway, albeit short-lived. Although their bill rolled through the Legislature, Davis once again interceded. After meeting with representatives of big business insurance companies in New York, the governor insisted that the bad faith bill be amended to exempt general business lawsuits, such as product liability cases, and be confined, in effect, to auto accident cases—thus impaling lawyers on their own propaganda, which had been that bad faith suits were needed to protect individual consumers against recalcitrant insurance companies in auto accidents and other similar matters. The effect of the amendment was to doom the legislation. Davis signed the measure in its revised form and immediately, the auto insurance industry pledged to spend as much as $50 million to defeat it in a referendum. The amendment exempting big business defendants and their insurers meant that the rich and powerful trial lawyer firms that specialized in multimillion-dollar cases against major corporations had no reason to put up the money to battle the auto insurers on the referendum. And the much smaller law firms that worked individual auto crash cases simply couldn't afford to pony up millions of dollars, or at least they couldn't be organized quickly enough as the referendum appeared on the March 2000, primary ballot.

The insurers' millions financed a massive and massively successful media campaign against the new law, attacking it as a tool for greedy lawyers, while the opposition effort was puny and misdirected. One example: The insurers carefully avoided any criticism of Davis as they attacked the law he signed while the lawyers angered the governor by invoking his name in their campaign materials. Davis didn't want any part of either side, having concluded that he had fulfilled his campaign pledge to the lawyers by signing the watered-down bad faith bill. The trial lawyers' bad faith law (technically, there were two laws and two referenda) was rejected by voters by a wide margin. Ultimately, the lawyers wound up with nothing to show for their concentrated drive in the 1999 legislative session—a demonstration of how lobbying must adapt to changing circumstances to be successful and the failure to adjust can be costly. One footnote: The lawyers' lobbyists made another stab at gaining the right to sue HMOs in 2000 with legislation that would prohibit binding arbitration in HMO care disputes, but were defeated inside the Assembly Democratic caucus, their bill dying without even a floor vote.

While the "napkin deal" is often cited as a classic example of how negotiations among interest group lobbyists and key legislators can bear fruit, the danger of such a closed-door process is that while it may result in something that can generate enough votes to be enacted, it may lack a structure that will hold up in the real world. No one who made the deal—including Willie Brown and Bill Lockyer—could envision, for example, that helping tobacco companies avoid personal injury lawsuits would become a political liability.

Recent history's most graphic example of an insider deal that backfired is the 1996 "deregulation" of California's privately owned electric utilities, principally Pacific Gas and Electric, Southern California Edison, and San Diego Gas and Electric. The push to break up the vertically integrated utilities and bring competition into the power market came from both the Federal Energy Regulatory Commission and the state Public Utilities Commission but key legislators, most notably San Diego's Senator Steve Peace, decided to enact their own version that would, they thought, be more palatable to the rate paying public. Weeks of private and quasi-public hearings and negotiations, dubbed the "Steve Peace death march" by one participant, resulted in a bill that would eventually result in deregulation, or so it was thought, but only after the utilities had been compensated for their "stranded costs" of old power plants, and rates had been frozen for a period. One feature of the scheme was a 10 percent rate cut financed by ratepayers through an easy-payment bond issue.

The plan was crafted to gain the support of the utilities and of big commercial and industrial power users who wanted to make their own deals with suppliers, with acquiescence of consumer groups. It succeeded brilliantly on that level and sailed through both houses of the Legislature without a dissenting vote in the dying hours of the 1996 legislative session, despite the misgivings of utility experts who saw it as a house of cards that could come tumbling down. A few years later, it began to disintegrate when utilities found themselves paying soaring wholesale prices for power on the spot market and precluded from passing those costs on to consumers. All of the assumptions on which the scheme was based turned out to be wrong and by early 2001, the utilities were on the verge of bankruptcy, having run up more than $12 billion in debts for power purchases in six months, and the state was forced to spend a billion dollars a month to buy power to keep California's lights burning while politicians scrambled to devise some longer-term solution to the crisis. What had seemed so clever in 1996 turned out to be an embarrassment for everyone involved. Peace was compelled to abandon his plans to run for statewide office because he was so personally identified with the failed scheme.

To lobbyists, however, there was a silver lining. Utilities, power generators, Wall Street bankers, big power users, and other interest groups shelled out millions of dollars in lobbying fees in 2001 as politicians grappled with the fallout, seeking the expertise of Capitol insiders to protect their huge financial stakes as some new system of electric power distribution was devised.

CHAPTER 4

Money, the Mother's Milk of Politics

*Money is the mother's milk of politics—Jesse Unruh, legendary
speaker of the California Assembly.*

On September 28, 1542, after an arduous, three-month voyage, two ships com-
manded by Spanish explorer Juan Cabrillo entered what he later described as a
"very good closed port." His shore party encountered a group of curious natives,
all but three of whom quickly fled as heavily armed and armored soldiers
landed. Cabrillo gave the trio a few trinkets.

The natural harbor Cabrillo discovered was San Diego Bay and his was the
first known encounter between whites and California's Indian population, which
modern scholars believe was 150,000 to 300,000 at the time, scattered among
dozens, if not hundreds, of tribes and clans, each with its own cultural and lin-
guistic characteristics and each having adapted to the widely varying climatic
and geographic conditions that, then as now, are two of California's unique at-
tributes.

The next four and a half centuries were cruel ones for California's Indians.
They were enslaved, slaughtered as vermin, driven off their traditional lands and
herded onto desolate reservations like so many animals, punished by white
overseers for speaking their languages or pursuing their religious customs,
starved by mining practices that destroyed fish and game, and felled by imported
diseases such as smallpox to which they had no natural resistance. It's a wonder
they survived at all, and they almost didn't, their numbers having dwindled to
about 15,000 souls, lashed by disease and abject poverty, by the end of the 19th
century. Genocide would not be too strong a word to describe what white set-

tlers, Catholic missionaries, gold miners, soldiers, and civil officials did to California's once-thriving Indian population during the centuries that followed contact with Cabrillo.

"The Indian was not kept in formal slavery, but he was exterminated at the wish and the expense of the Legislature, and for years in the southern part of the state, under the guise of penal labor, Indians were hawked from the auction-block," historian Kevin Starr wrote of 19th century California's treatment of its native residents.

The late 19th century and early 20th century brought some relief to California Indians. The activism of such reformers as novelist Helen Hunt Jackson ended the cruelest treatment of Indians, but they still languished in poverty and despair on their marginal reservation lands, largely ignored and left to fend for themselves as the state propelled itself into the auto-borne, industrial era. "Never in the poorest huts of the most poverty-stricken wilds of Italy, Bavaria, Norway and New Mexico," Jackson wrote, had she seen anything "so loathsome as the kennels in which some of the San Diego Indians are living."

By the 1960s, the tiny, impoverished Santa Rosa Indian rancheria in the San Joaquin Valley southwest of Fresno had seen only one of its residents ever graduate from high school. The graduate was promptly drafted into the military and sent to Vietnam, where he was killed within a few months. But the lives of those who weren't drafted were, on average, decades shorter than whites as Indian communities were ravaged by poor health care, alcoholism and other chronic diseases. As late as the 1980s, California Indians had virtually no influence in the Capitol. Legislators with Indian reservations in their districts would occasionally introduce legislation dealing with health care or some other issues but it rarely became law. Indians didn't have any money, they didn't have a lobbyist; and they didn't vote much. Barbara Gonzales Lyons, a leader of the Agua Caliente Band of Cahuilla Indians, recalled in a 2000 newspaper interview, "Nobody took notice of us before, and our issues were never addressed in Sacramento because we were not able to lobby before. Ten years ago, we didn't even have the funds to take care of our people, much less donate to campaigns." State officials tended to consider Indians, if they thought of them at all, as the responsibility of the federal government, which had created the extensive system of reservations and rancherias in the 19th century and had an entire department supposedly looking after Indian interests.

The final decade of the 20th century saw California Indian tribes assert themselves and within a few years become perhaps the most powerful political force in the nation's most populous state, using the non-Indian population's own money, funneled through tribal gambling casinos, to buy unmatched access and influence in a Legislature that once declared them to be pests. The meteoric rise of Indians from a powerless, ignored, and relatively tiny segment of California society into masters of the political universe presents the most dramatic case study of how money—cold cash delivered into the right pockets—plays a central role in deciding what and what does not happen in the Capitol, especially when the issues themselves are dripping with monetary consequences and hired-gun lobbyists are dueling in the back hallways, validating the old saying "money talks and bullshit walks."

California's political and economic interest groups spend well over a quarter-billion dollars on "political action" every year, the money paying the fees of Capitol lobbyists, hiring political consultants and public relations experts, and flowing into the campaign coffers of officeholders and those who want to be. That sounds like a lot of cash, and it is by the standards of anyone not named Bill Gates, but compared to the stakes involved in winning or losing battles in the Capitol, it's chicken feed. The decisions that official Sacramento makes, from the passage or defeat of legislation to which drug is approved for administration to poor people under the state's Medi-Cal program, can be worth 100 times as much as the political money being expended. And the prospect of a 10,000 percent profit from an investment in politics draws interest groups to Sacramento like flies to carrion.

To cite but one example: In the 1980s, a consulting firm that specializes in writing ballot measures proposed to an organization of service station and garage owners that it sponsor a law requiring every motorist in California to have his or her car subjected to a regular safety inspection, much like they are required to have their smog-control systems checked and certified. The consulting firm calculated how much income would be generated for the garages by compelling the owners of 20-plus million vehicles and compared it to the cost of qualifying and passing the ballot measure, demonstrating the potential for profits in the 100-to-1 range. The effort collapsed, but the proposal—a kind of prospectus for a political stock issue—indicated the mindset that permeates the political process. Had it succeeded, the drive would have netted the consulting firm millions of dollars in fees for managing the campaign. Is it any wonder that the drive to create a $2 billion-per-year state lottery was conceived and financed by a company that produces lottery materials and won the initial contract for California's lottery?

A similar attitude surrounds legislation in the Capitol. Lawmakers know that the passage or defeat of a particular bill could mean many millions, perhaps even billions, of dollars in some interest group's pocket. At the very least, they reason, those soliciting their votes should be willing to share some of the bounty by making regular contributions to their campaign treasuries as a kind of entrance fee to play the game. Some politicians are more explicit than others in demanding the gate fee, but everyone involved in these delicate transactions know that a precise quid pro quo arrangement connecting a campaign check to a vote is illegal bribery, so all sorts of euphemistic phrases make their way into the conversations, some of which are conducted by legislative aides or campaign consultants to add a layer of insulation, or deniability.

Lobbyists know, for instance, that members of key committees are likely to send out invitations to fundraising events a week or two before the committees are to handle their heaviest agendas of bills, deciding whether they will live or die. And, of course, the lobbyists know that timing can be everything when they advise their clients to whom they should send checks, how much they should send, and when they should send it. Whether it's a shakedown, as some lobbyists say privately, or legalized bribery, as reformers contend publicly, it's a system that's evolved and refined itself over several decades.

When pioneer lobbyist Artie Samish was perfecting his "select and elect" system during the 1930s and 1940s to create a Legislature friendly to his clients, he didn't have to spend very much money by modern standards, even after the numbers are adjusted for the cost of living. A few hundred dollars, a few thousand at most, were enough to win a state Assembly seat in those days. In his highly entertaining, and highly revealing, autobiography, *The Secret Boss of California,* Samish describes how an operative went to skid row in downtown Los Angeles in 1934, picked out one of the down-and-outers, bought him some new clothes for $25, spent another $10 for a bath, shave, and haircut, and paid a fee to have him listed as a Democratic candidate in the district of a veteran assemblyman that Samish wanted to rattle on behalf of a client. Samish then had 100,000 cards printed with the picture of the "candidate" and set him to work passing them out in the district, paying him $10 a day to campaign for himself. To the surprise of everyone, the former bum's grassroots campaign caught fire and he won, defeating a seemingly entrenched incumbent, and Samish had himself a friendly legislator for a cost of about $2,000, including the new clothes. "He wasn't a bad legislator at all," Samish wrote decades later. "He had a degree of intelligence and he voted according to his conscience . . . always for poor, the downtrodden." The bum-turned-legislator lived frugally, actually getting by on the position's $100 per month salary, and served a decade in Sacramento before dying.

Through the 1940s and 1950s, running for and retaining legislative seats was still a fairly inexpensive business. Most legislators and candidates were able to raise the few thousand dollars they needed for billboards, sound trucks, and radio and newspaper ads from friends and local fundraising events, such as crab feeds and spaghetti dinners. Sacramento lobbyists might have arranged for some contributions but they didn't play huge roles in deciding who won which office, the Samish system notwithstanding. Their influence was felt in other ways, especially in the lavish wining and dining that became a way of life, and in the after-hours carousing that an almost entirely male Legislature and an entirely male lobbying corps enjoyed together.

Dramatic change came in the 1960s with Jesse Unruh and the full-time, professional Legislature. Unruh wanted to build his own organization that would decide who was elected—based on loyalty to Unruh—and although he had said the full-time Legislature would be a bulwark against special interest influence, in effect it institutionalized and systematized the financial relationships between those who wanted something to happen for their clients and those who could make it happen. Full-time, professional legislators were more money-centered than their quasi-amateur predecessors because the personal stakes in winning or losing campaigns were higher. And Unruh and other modern legislative leaders, at least until term limits produced another cultural change in the 1990s, wanted money to flow through their hands, or those of trusted lieutenants, to put them in the position to select candidates and anoint them with the money they needed to win. One Unruh protégé, Willie Brown, even instituted what was called "tithing"—those on whom he bestowed committee chairmanships or other leadership positions were expected to raise money from the interest groups with whom they dealt and shift a certain amount of it to Brown. Brown spent the money on targeted districts to elect Brown-loyal candidates and strengthen his grip on the speakership, a form of the "select and elect" strategy that Samish invented.

While Unruh presented a public case for professionalization of the Legislature—saying it would blunt the influence of special interests—neither he nor his successors ever publicly acknowledged that professionalization would lead to centralization and its attendant effects.

Professionalization and centralization escalated the amount of money raised for legislative campaigns because it increased the level of partisan competition for control of the Legislature and, eventually, factional infighting such as the year-long struggle in 1980 between two groups of Democrats for control of the Assembly speakership, a battle financed by special interest groups. And much of the money was often spent by professional legislators for expenses not directly related to campaigning, with campaign treasuries being treated as private slush funds to finance meals, travel, clothes and other living expenses, even though they received tax-free "per diem" payments to cover their expenses from the state in addition to salaries. Two of countless examples of odd use of campaign funds illustrate the syndrome. Barry Keene, a Democratic state senator of the 1970s and 1980s, used campaign funds to pay his psychiatric counseling bills. A contemporary Republican senator, Jim Nielsen, put his second wife on his campaign payroll with a salary almost exactly equal to what Nielsen was paying his first wife in alimony and child support, and neglected to report the extra family income until a newspaper reporter wrote about the strange coincidence.

Keene, as it happens, was also part of a milestone in campaign fundraising and spending in 1972 when he and his Democratic opponent for an Assembly seat each spent more than $100,000—the first time an Assembly campaign had reached that amount. Much of the money to finance the contest between Keene and Gary Antolini on California's sprawling North Coast came from party leaders in Sacramento because they believed control of the Assembly would hinge on the outcome. At the time, it was still not uncommon for politicians to spend $15,000–$20,000 to win a legislative campaign, but those days were about to change forever. In the early 1980s, former antiwar activist Tom Hayden spent more than a million dollars to win a Los Angeles Assembly seat, by the late 1980s, legislative campaigns were averaging $1 million a seat, and by 1998, two candidates for Keene's old Senate seat on the sparsely populated, heavily forested North Coast spent more than $5 million each, the Republican financed by his family's winemaking fortune, the Democrat by party leaders in Sacramento. One couldn't raise that kind of money with spaghetti feeds.

Campaign fundraising was concentrated in Sacramento in the late 1970s and early 1980s—except for the occasional wealthy, self-financed candidate such as Hayden or the little old winemaker—and lobbyists in the third house found themselves showered by a daily cascade of invitations to breakfasts, luncheons, and dinners, staged either in Sacramento or in the politician's district. Fundraisers became so common that some lobbyists logged them into computer spreadsheets to keep track of who was asking for what. A cottage industry developed in Sacramento in the design and execution of events, from the format of the invitations to the brand and vintage of the wine and the shape of ice-sculptures on reception tables bearing shrimp and vegetables. Golf tournaments, fishing expeditions, and other events were cooked up as facades for putting the arm on lobbyists and their clients. As soon as Sacramento acquired a Triple A baseball team in 2000, Capitol politicians rented luxury suites at the new ballpark and invited lobbyists to watch the games—for a price, of course. Senator Bruce McPherson used a friend's home on the fairway of a Pebble Beach golf course to host fundraising events during the annual golf tournament formerly known as the "Crosby Clambake." Senator Liz Figueroa threw a 50th birthday party for herself at a Maui resort in 2001 and charged lobbyists $1,050 to attend.

Lobbyists munched on the giant shrimp, sipped the vintage wines, picked at the eggs Benedict, teed up for the golf tournaments, and oiled their fishing gear. But they understood that it was all just for show. The real game was how much money they could raise from their clients and how it would be parceled out among the pleaders, based on the glinty-eyed calculation of which politician had been friendly to their clients' interests, or would be likely to favor those interests in the future. And the cumulative effect of those decisions largely determines the makeup of the Legislature before any votes are cast. If lobbyists are keeping score on one end, they know that beneath the superficial bonhomie, the politicians are keeping accounts as well. More than one lobbyist who sought access to a legislator has found himself answering the question, "Did you get an invitation to my fundraiser?" Freshmen Assembly members demand $750 or more to attend an event, and, for legislative leaders, it can be $2,000 or more—an entire $20,000 table.

Ironically, one of the biggest spurs to the escalation of political fundraising has been a ballot measure that was billed as a reform to lessen lobbyist influence on Sacramento—Proposition 9, the Political Reform Act, approved by voters in 1974 as a state-level response to the Watergate scandal in Washington. Proposition 9's prohibition on lobbyists' making or arranging for campaign contributions was set aside by the courts as an abridgment of free speech, the same legal shoals on which other reform programs have foundered. Left intact, however, was Proposition 9's requirement for more frequent and complete reporting of campaign contributions, as well as gifts from interest groups to politicians. Proposition 9 campaign reports filled the role that reformers envisioned, giving media and the public a better picture of who was giving to whom and thus the opportunity to relate contributions to votes on bills. But the reports also gave politicians a window into the fundraising of their personal, factional, and/or partisan rivals and hard evidence with which to confront special interest groups and their lobbyists to demand parity. Legislative leaders and their campaign consultants developed detailed, cross-referenced books on who was giving and who was receiving and were known to admonish lobbyists for groups deemed to be insufficiently generous. The maintenance and use of such a log became a factor in the conviction of one former state senator, Paul Carpenter, on federal bribery charges. The Proposition 9 reports also provided lobbyists with information about what their rivals were doing and allowed them to refine their strategies for passing or defeating bills on behalf of clients.

The game reached its zenith in the 1980s as an anything-goes mentality gripped the Capitol with Assembly Speaker Willie Brown seemingly setting the tone. One scandal erupted in the early 1980s, surrounding the efforts by a fireworks manufacturer to enact a state statute barring local anti-fireworks ordinances. One legislator was convicted of mail fraud in the influence-peddling scandal but others narrowly escaped indictment. The conviction was overturned on appeal, and the politician involved returned to the Capitol as a lobbyist. It should have been a wake-up call that the FBI—which had briefly investigated the Capitol in the 1970s—was very interested in what happened inside the building. But the wheeler-dealer atmosphere that Brown fostered continued—until federal agents, ending a years-long undercover investigation of Capitol influence-peddling, swooped into the Capitol with subpoenas and search warrants, scooping up boxes of material from legislators' and lobbyists' files and revealing that they had videotaped legislators, legislative staffers, and others systematically shaking down investigators posing as businessmen seeking special tax breaks for a mythical shrimp processing plant. The shakedowns involved both campaign funds and personal payments in the guise of "honoraria" for speeches never delivered, and eventually a number of Capitol figures, including the aforementioned Paul Carpenter, were convicted and clapped into federal prison for lengthy stretches. Many lobbyists and lawmakers who didn't get indicted breathed sighs of relief because they knew they had participated in transactions every bit as explicit as the ones that sent colleagues to prison.

The FBI sting led to a few superficial reforms, such as a ban on honoraria and other forms of personal income, and fed the drive for legislative term limits. It made participants in the Capitol game a little warier of how they conduct business. When it was revealed that some Capitol types had worn radio transmitters to ensnare others after being snagged by the investigation, handshake greetings sometimes included a quick hand down the back to check for wires beneath suit jackets. But neither the scandal nor term limits changed the fundamental game—the governor, legislators, and other officials make decisions with multi-billion-dollar consequences, and one of the ways those decisions are influenced is to contribute lavishly to campaign treasuries of the decision makers. Voter-approved limits on campaign contributions were largely gutted by the courts on free speech grounds, although the Legislature itself placed on the 2000 ballot a relatively weak measure imposing limits on campaign contributions. As the century turned, the identities of the interest groups leading the political arms race had evolved, but money was still talking and bullshit was still walking. When the professional era of the Legislature began in the 1960s and 1970s, the Capitol's big money players were still pretty much who they had been during the previous several decades, such as Artie Samish's old clients, the liquor and horse racing industries. Fair trade laws might have been largely voided by the courts, but the various segments of the liquor industry—beer, wine, and hard liquor distributors, particularly—still carried big sticks in the Capitol. Sacramento's most prominent lobbyist, in fact, was "The Judge," former judge and legislator James Garibaldi, whose lobbying practice was an adjunct of former Governor Pat Brown's southern California law firm and whose chief clients were wine and liquor distributors and horse racing interests. It was generally acknowledged that The Judge could get almost anything he wanted from the two legislative committees that handled liquor, gambling, and other "sin" legislation, and what his clients wanted was what they had wanted when Samish represented them: state-enforced monopolies and minimal taxation.

At the time, the horse tracks had a near-lock on legal gambling in California and state law, closely monitored by Garibaldi and other equine lobbyists, delineated which breeds of horses could race on which days at which tracks, thus preventing competition from rearing its ugly head. Some folks talked about off-track betting or legalizing dog racing tracks like those in Arizona, but the horsemen and their lobbyists beat back every attempt at either—although they eventually agreed to a form of off-track betting in which the wagers had to be placed at the tracks themselves on races at other tracks in California and other states, thereby effectively preserving the monopoly. It was a mark of Garibaldi's influence in the 1970s that he was able to secure a $100-plus million per year tax break for the tracks—on the unproved assertion that they were facing bleak economic times—during a period when the governor of the era, Jerry Brown, was rejecting appropriations for libraries because, he said, the state was strapped for cash. "Millions for bookies, nothing for books" was the headline on one critical article about the dichotomy. Administration officials insisted that Brown's signature on the tax break bill had nothing to do with the fact that his father's law firm represented the state's largest track and employed the courtly Garibaldi as its Sacramento lobbyist.

The Judge also effectively represented his liquor clients, especially the Wine and Spirit Wholesalers of California, in a years-long drive to restore parts of the old liquor "fair trade laws" that Samish had installed but the courts had shredded in the 1970s as monopolistic, anti-consumer price-fixing schemes. Voiding Samish's liquor laws introduced price competition into the huge California liquor trade and beginning in the late 1970s, within months of the courts' action, Garibaldi began a series of legislative efforts to reinstate them piecemeal, often working hand-in-glove with Ralph Dills, another legendary figure in the Capitol (first elected to the Legislature in 1938) and for many years chairman of the Senate Governmental Organization Committee or "GO" to Capitol insiders, and Frank Vicencia, chairman of the Assembly GO Committee. The GO committees of both houses were considered at the time to be the top-ranked "juice committees," and legislators schemed constantly to win GO seats, knowing that membership brought an automatic bounty of campaign contributions from liquor, horse racing, and other gambling interests, such as the state's poker parlors, which could operate with local government approval.

Garibaldi's initial efforts to bring back fair trade laws succeeded because Jerry Brown either signed the bills that The Judge shepherded through a Legislature eager to do his bidding or allowed them to become law without his signature. The bills restricted price competition in liquor, although beer wholesalers, who were not represented by Garibaldi, had a tougher time of it than Garibaldi's clients—who also happened to be Pat Brown's law clients. Garibaldi found the going much tougher after Republican George Deukmejian succeeded Brown in 1983, and his clients sought legislative approval of a measure imposing curbs on unrestricted imports of wine and champagne, facing stiff opposition from grocery store and discount liquor chains. It took a direct intercession by Assembly Speaker Willie Brown to save the Garibaldi/Dills measure after a strong coalition of free-enterprise Republicans and proconsumer liberal Democrats threatened its approval by the Assembly Ways and Means Committee. Brown's intervention, changing the votes of two liberal Democrats, may have had something to do with his ties to Henry Berman, a top San Francisco political fundraiser and a "consultant" to the Seagram liquor empire, a major vintner that wanted protection from foreign competition and was backing the Dills bill. But neither Garibaldi nor Brown could save the bill from a veto by Deukmejian, who said it would increase liquor prices to consumers by limiting competition in imported products.

Deukmejian's 1986 veto of Senate Bill 599, the wine import restriction measure, was not only a setback for The Judge and his clients, but marked the beginning of a turnaround in the Capitol's hierarchy of interests. The old-line lobbies such as liquor and horse racing were giving way to a new batch of players and a new generation of lobbyists who were learning to play the high-stakes money game. The liquor trade itself was changing, some forms becoming less popular with consumers concerned about health effects and drunken driving—

the latter symbolized by Candy Lightner's antidrunken driving campaign—and horse racing track attendance and wagering were dropping as younger Californians looked for thrills and gambling opportunities in other venues, such as the state's new lottery, expanding local card rooms, and easily accessible super-casinos in Las Vegas. New players in the gambling trade, Indian-owned casinos, were just beginning to make themselves known and just beginning to buy their way into political hegemony in the Capitol. By the end of the 1990s—and the end of the century—the Capitol's most influential special interests, as measured by their political action expenditures and their success in winning favors, were for the most part groups that didn't exist a quarter-century earlier. They included health care providers, particularly the huge health maintenance organizations, public employee unions such as the powerhouse California Correctional Peace Officers Association and the California Teachers Association, and the Indian-owned casinos, which were generating billions of wagering dollars each year.

The roots of that phenomenal growth of Indian casinos are to be found in the out-of-sight-out-of-mind condition to which Indians were relegated in the 19th and 20th centuries, after the most egregious forms of repression, virtually genocide, stopped. For the most part, Indian reservations and rancherias were located on the most unproductive lands that government officials could find, thwarting any ambitions Indians might have to engage in traditional agriculture or hunting. Government handouts kept California Indians alive, but barely. In desperation, a few tribes opened bingo parlors in hopes of attracting some money, contending that since they were considered sovereign nations, they didn't need state authority for bingo. That touched off a legal war that resulted in a lawsuit involving the Cabazon Indians in the southern California desert that reached the Supreme Court in 1987 and produced a big win for the tribes. The decision held, in effect, that there were no legal restrictions on Indian gambling.

Casinos, many of them in shabby temporary buildings because the Indians lacked capital, began to appear on tribal lands, particularly those closest to major highways cutting through the desert, and Congress responded with the Indian Gaming Regulatory Act (IGRA) of 1988, which professed—but largely failed—to bring some legal clarity to the situation. In essence, IGRA divided gambling into three categories or classes, ranging from social gambling of the sort conducted by charities, to minor games such as bingo and pull-tabs, and finally to full-fledged, Nevada-style gambling, including slot machines. Indians were authorized by IGRA to conduct gambling of the same class otherwise allowed in the state if they had negotiated "compacts" with the states in which they operated, a condition that touched off years of legal wrangling and high-stakes political action over what, exactly, was legal. The political war focused almost entirely on slot machines, especially the modern, computerized video games that are the single most popular form of gambling and a guaranteed profit center. The payoffs are adjustable, and they don't need human operators like blackjack and other forms of casino gambling.

Indians contended that they had a legal right to own slot machines because the state sanctioned other forms of "Class III" gambling such as poker parlors and betting on horse races. But antigambling groups, law enforcement agencies, rivals for the gamblers' dollars, in California and Nevada, considered the slots to be illegal—a position taken by two Republican governors, George Deukmejian and Pete Wilson. The U.S. Department of Justice regularly threatened to raid the Indian casinos but held back while the issue was thrashed out in the civil courts and the political arena. California Indians were playing for time and as money poured into their new, larger, and more elaborate casinos, they hired top-drawer legal and political talent and became big-time players in the Capitol's own political casino.

Indians pumped money into legislative campaigns during the 1990s, spreading it to politicians of both parties but concentrating on Democrats, and learned that—as tribal leader Barbara Gonzales Lyons observed—the money bought them the political respect they could never achieve when they were poor. A stalemate developed in the mid-1990s, with Governor Wilson insisting he would not negotiate compacts with tribes to end the legal uncertainty until they shut down their slot machines, and the Indians packing as many customers as possible into their casinos and building up their financial and political reserves. Clinton's Justice Department also stalled for time, refusing Wilson's repeated requests to crack down on the slot machines he and the department both said were illegal.

By the late 1990s, roughly half of California's 100 Indian reservations and rancherias had some form of gambling, ranging from tiny bingo parlors to huge, Nevada-style casino resort-hotels with entertainment. While precise numbers are impossible to obtain from the secretive casinos, it's estimated that Indian casinos are generating about $4 billion a year in gross gaming revenues. And they are, in the time-honored fashion of the Capitol, sharing that wealth with politicians in the form of campaign contributions. Statistics compiled by California Common Cause and released in 2000 demonstrate the growth in Indian political giving, from $78,117 in 1995 to $7.3 million in 1998—not counting the tens of millions of dollars the tribes spent to pass two ballot measures that finally legalized their slot machines and forced the powerful Nevada casinos to wave the white flag and seek a peace treaty that would allow them to get in on the Indian action. The top tribal contributor during the 1995–98 period was the Morongo Band of Mission Indians, which operates a large casino adjacent to Interstate 10 between Riverside and Palm Springs, at $1.7 million, but two other casino tribes topped $1 million.

Late in his governorship, Wilson negotiated a series of compacts with tribes that wanted to launch gambling, but hadn't yet done so. Wilson hailed the "Pala compact," named for one of the tribes in southern California, as a model that would allow modest expansion of Indian gambling but impose some limits. The compact allowed a form of slot machine that technically, Wilson and others maintained, would not violate state laws generally barring slots. But the larger tribes already operating casinos despised the new compacts as limiting their ability to expand and vowed to take the ratifying state legislation to the ballot as a referendum, while promoting a rival ballot measure that would, in effect, give Indians a monopoly on slot machines in California. The battle over the latter, Proposition 5, in 1998, reached epic proportions with the tribes and their foes— Nevada casinos, horse racing tracks, poker parlors, and the hotel and restaurant workers union—spending about $100 million on campaigns that saturated the air waves with TV spots.

The casino Indians won big at the polls. Their ballot measure was approved handily as voters responded to their highly effective TV ads, most of which portrayed gambling as the means by which Indians had lifted themselves out of abject poverty, and Democrat Gray Davis, a supporter of Indian casinos, defeated gambling foe Dan Lungren for the governorship. The Indians' across-the-board victory was marred only by a state Supreme Court decision voiding the ballot measure's provisions. But in a stark demonstration of the tribes' political clout, Davis "negotiated" a series of compacts giving Indians pretty much all they wanted in gambling authority. He and state legislators quickly enacted a constitutional amendment to ratify the new pacts and overcome the judicial problems, a measure that was ratified by voters in March 2000.

The Indians' chief political opponents, the Nevada casinos, conceded after the first ballot measure passed overwhelmingly. Instead of fighting the second one, they eagerly sought contracts from tribes to operate the lavish new casinos that were launched within weeks of the second measure's approval. With a monopoly on legal slot machines in the nation's most populous state, tribes could entertain offers of development capital from banking interests. Although Davis insisted that the compacts he awarded the tribes would allow only a "modest" expansion of slots to about 44,000, the Legislature's budget office pegged the ceiling at well over 100,000, thus creating the potential for a tribal gambling industry of many billions of dollars a year.

The first of the Nevada-style slots were installed in Indian casinos within three months of the second ballot measure, and a University of Nevada professor who specializes in the economics of gambling told an industry convention in Las Vegas that Indian casinos in California could surpass the revenues of those in Nevada by 2010, terming it a "scary proposition" for the Nevada gaming industry. Prof. Bill Eadington noted that as much as a third of southern Nevada's gambling base comes from southern California while the Reno-Tahoe casinos are even more dependent on gamblers from northern California. Eadington said by 2010, California's Indian casinos could be generating from $5.1 billion to $10.3 billion, the latter more than twice the volume of the Las Vegas strip. In late 2000, just before leaving the White House, President Bill Clinton signed a bill granting an obscure Sonoma County Indian tribe the right to acquire a large and financially marginal poker parlor in San Pablo, on the east side of San Francisco Bay and a few yards from Interstate 80. The legislation effectively allowed the Indians to convert the card room into a full-fledged casino, complete with slot machines—the first to be established in a major urban area, seemingly opening a new chapter in the evolution of Indian gambling in the state. The huge new California gambling industry results directly from the application of money to the process, a massive amount by political standards but a tiny fraction of what the Indian casinos are likely to realize from their phenomenally successful political action campaign.

The tribes' few remaining rivals, meanwhile, were left gasping by this political blitzkrieg. Although the horseracing tracks and poker parlors remained, by conventional standards, major sources of campaign money, their contributions paled in comparison and they found themselves fighting for their lives in a Capitol they had owned just a decade earlier. The same judicial decision that set aside the Indians' first ballot measure placed a legal cloud on the cardrooms' newer games, designed to serve new markets such as Asian gamblers. It forced their lobbyists to seek legislation that would, they hoped, stop the hemorrhage of customers to the newer, bigger, flashier and more comprehensive Indian gambling palaces popping up all over the state, including some on the fringes of major urban areas. The poker parlor lobbyists managed to get one bill through the process and to Davis's desk but he vetoed it. The tribes made it clear to the Capitol that they didn't want to allow their rivals to get off the floor. And in early 2001, a coalition of San Francisco Bay Area card room operators, seeing the San Pablo casino as a death knell for their industry, filed a federal lawsuit to overturn all of California's pro-Indian gambling laws, saying they went beyond the simple equity that Congress intended to impose on the states. A small item in Davis's $5-plus billion transportation program, unveiled in 2000, demonstrated the hegemony the Indians had achieved. It allocated $30 million in state transportation funds to build a new interchange on Interstate 10 to funnel gamblers into the Morongo Band's casino, even though local transportation authorities said it wasn't on their list of projects to relieve traffic congestion in the fast-growing Inland Empire. Shortly after the $30 million was included in the program, the Morongos contributed $35,000 to Davis's campaign treasury.

Lobbyists, as well as politicians, profited from the Indians' massive involvement in Capitol politics. Despite their general agreement on expanding Indian gambling, the tribes often disagreed among themselves on details and, as any lobbyist knows, there's financial opportunity in conflict. Different tribes or tribal groups hired their own lobbyists to pursue their particular interests, while the cardrooms and horseracing tracks beefed up lobbying and campaign giving in a largely vain effort to keep up with their Indian rivals. The tribes did much of their lobbying themselves, regularly filling Capitol hearings rooms with Indians to reinforce their contention that gambling is the "new buffalo" that would provide them with much-needed financial strength. And despite their successes, there is no indication that the Indians will retire from the political battlefield because the struggle over control of gambling in California is likely to continue for years as the white-owned cardrooms and horseracing tracks pursue what they believe is a fight for survival either in the courts, alleging that the Indian monopoly on slot machines violates federal law, or in the political arena. The assumption in the Capitol is that full-scale casino gambling is a certainty in California and the Indians may enjoy an initial monopoly, but the amounts of money involved are just too vast for others to simply accept that as a fact and fade away. Ironically, as the casino tribes became a huge source of campaign funds, their status as semi-autonomous governments created a legal dilemma. Other governments were barred by law from making campaign contributions, but the Indians claimed an exemption that no one was willing to challenge in the courts. The tribes contended that they didn't even have to file campaign contribution reports with the state, but did so only as a friendly gesture.

The casino tribes' meteoric rise was only the most spectacular example of how the hierarchy of interest group power changed during the final two decades of the century. The parallel ascendance of public employee unions, particularly the huge prison guards union, is only slightly less impressive. It began—as did the Indians' rise—with a political decision, in this case the enactment of collective bargaining for California's city, county, school, and state workers in the late 1970s, thanks to the absolute control that union-friendly Democrats enjoyed in the Capitol at that moment. But it also took two other political acts to make the public worker unions' power as massive as it eventually became: the passage of Proposition 13 in 1978 and, almost concurrently, the enactment of a series of tough-on-crime laws that pushed tens of thousands of new inmates into the state's prison system and forced the state to build dozens of new prisons and spend heavily on thousands of new guards and other employees.

A major effect of Proposition 13, perhaps unintended, was to shift primary responsibility for financing local governments, particularly counties, and schools from locally elected boards and councils to the governor and the Legislature. The concentration of financial decision making in Sacramento was the impetus for the newly franchised public employee unions to concentrate their political activities on Capitol politicians who held the pursestrings, although the unions also gained tremendous authority in local governments and schools, especially in major urban areas. The Sacramento focus was symbolized by the California Teachers Association's decision to buy a building near the Capitol that had once housed a restaurant popular with politicians and lobbyists and convert it into a political headquarters with a faint resemblance to a Spanish colonial schoolhouse.

The CTA and other big public worker unions became a major source of campaign funds, almost entirely for Democrats, during the 1980s. It paid off handsomely because Republicans held the governorship for 16 years in the 1980s and 1990s and the unions could count on the Democrats to protect their interests, especially when a major recession hit the state during the early 1990s requiring wholesale cuts in spending. One months-long stalemate on the state budget centered on a dispute between Governor Pete Wilson and the CTA over school financing. The tens of millions of dollars that the CTA and other public unions invested in politics during the final two decades of the century generated huge returns when Democrat Davis took over the governorship during a period of prosperity, with billions of tax dollars flowing into the state treasury. Many of those billions were funneled back to the schools—although not to local governments—particularly after the CTA reminded Davis of its power by threatening to pursue a ballot measure forcing the state to spend heavily on schools, a followup to the 1988 CTA-backed measure (Proposition 98) that guaranteed a basic state financing package for education. With the CTA's financial clout evident in ballot measures and in the Capitol, public education easily became the largest single item in the state budget, consuming about 40 percent of its general fund. Most of those new dollars flowed into teachers' salaries because of the unions' ability to elect friendly school board members at the local level, filling a vacuum that was created when local civic and business interests abandoned school governance after Proposition 13 removed the school boards' power to set tax rates.

The California Correctional Peace Officers Association (CCPOA), meanwhile, was fashioning a political powerhouse of its own, again symbolized by a building, a fancy new headquarters in West Sacramento. From 20,000 inmates in 1980, the state prison system expanded rapidly to 160,000 in 2000, while Department of Corrections spending ballooned from $400 million to $4 billion and its payroll from about 9,000 to 45,000 workers—virtually all of them potential CCPOA members. Former prison guard Don Novey assumed the CCPOA's presidency and established himself, among hard-to-impress Capitol professionals, as an organizational and tactical genius. He didn't hesitate to spend millions on politicians he thought would further the union's goals: tougher laws to clap more felons behind bars and more prisons, requiring more guards, to house the inmates.

Just as the CTA capitalized on the public's regard for schools, Novey and the CCPOA took advantage of California's affinity for tough crime laws, one that sharpened during the 1980s and 1990s even as violent crime rates were falling after hitting a peak about 1980. Lurid media treatment of crime stories and a drumbeat of propaganda from politicians and anticrime groups fueled the public's fervor for tougher crime laws, such as "three-strikes-and-you're out," that would lock up more felons. Novey played a political masterstroke by funneling CCPOA money into "victims' rights" groups that would supply witnesses for legislative hearings on crime bills, telling tearful, made-for-television stories of how they or their loved ones had been victimized. CCPOA provided seed money for Fresno photographer Mike Reynolds' drive to enact the "three-strikes-and-you're-out" initiative. It was a very sophisticated and very effective grassroots organization that played perfectly into CCPOA's lobbying work inside the Capitol. Politicians could be on the popular side of an emotional issue—crime—and be compensated in the form of generous campaign checks. Few resisted the temptation. The only ones who did were liberals from safe urban districts.

Novey demonstrated his genius for timing by adroitly shifting from party to party. His is one of the few public employee unions to give generously to Republicans as well as Democrats, reflecting the GOP's love of tough crime bills and the Democrats' support for bread-and-butter labor issues. The guards gave Republican Pete Wilson a million dollars when he ran for governor in 1990 and eight years later bankrolled Democrat Gray Davis with $2.3 million. They backed a winner each time and it paid off in continuing pressure from the governor's office on an often reluctant Legislature to build more prisons and hire more guards, who would, in turn, pay more dues to the CCPOA and generate more campaign money. During the same election year in which it was backing Davis, CCPOA became the single largest contributor of legislative campaign funds at $1.8 million. Overall, the union spends at least $5 million every election cycle on campaign contributions to candidates and ballot measures. The CCPOA even formed what Common Cause called "a most unusual alliance" in 1998 with the Indian tribes, founding the Native Americans and Peace Officers PAC to make independent expenditures on Davis's behalf, although the bulk of the money came from three casino tribes.

"While the groups have seemingly unrelated political objectives," Common Cause said in a 2000 report on Indian political contributions, "they practice remarkably similar political strategies. In fact, the tribes' emergence as a major political donor mimics the strategy so successfully pioneered by the prison guards. It includes spending heavily on behalf of the winning gubernatorial candidate and lavishing substantial contributions on virtually all sitting legislators of both parties. This approach forsakes the partisan giving of many interest groups and instead seeks to maximize effectiveness by currying favor with all decision makers."

CCPOA has become a complete political organization. A source of lavish campaign contributions, it employs a squad of well-connected lobbyists, both staffers and contract lobbyists, lawyers who represent prison guards in their dealings with prison management, and public relations experts who drive home the message that prison guards walk "the toughest beat in the state" and should be rewarded handsomely by taxpayers.

With the CCPOA backing Davis, his support among public employee unions was virtually complete in 1998. In addition to the $2.3 million from the guards, Davis received another $1.2 million from the CTA, about a third of the money that the teachers union spread among candidates in 1998. The CTA sealed its position as one of the state's political money heavyweights by pumping another $17 million into ballot measures. It contributed heavily to organized labor's $20 million campaign to defeat a Pete Wilson-backed ballot measure that would have crippled unions' ability to raise political money from their members, and it helped pass a $9.2 billion school construction bond issue. Davis got another $1.1 million from the California State Employees Association (CSEA), which yearned for a Democratic governor after 16 years of Republican austerity. All of the public employee unions that backed Davis cashed in their chits in 1999 and 2000 as the new governor, enjoying a state treasury brimming with cash, handed out hefty raises and new retirement benefits, backed construction of new prison cells, and diverted several extra billion dollars into school systems, most of which would go into teachers' raises, although it took the threat of a CTA-backed ballot measure to finally secure the latter.

At century's end, the Indian tribes and public employee unions sat atop the political pyramid in Sacramento by dint of their ability and willingness to raise and spend immense sums, the kind of money that politicians couldn't imagine just a few years earlier. A *Los Angeles Times* compilation revealed that a half-billion dollars were spent on state political campaigns in 1998, including ballot measures, and that 330 corporations, labor unions, trade associations, and individuals accounted for about 60 percent of the total with 48 of the 330 giving $1 million or more and eight $10 million or more. Everyone in the Capitol knew, based on what happened in 1999 and 2000, that it had been money well spent, that billions of dollars in state spending, gambling proceeds and other financial rewards flowed to the big spenders.

While new financial power centers were developing in and around the Capitol during the 1990s, the direction of campaign money was changing subtly, largely because of legislative term limits. As the power of legislative leaders to control campaign money and anoint candidates waned, lobbyists—or at least those sophisticated enough to understand that times had changed—began reasserting themselves as active players in shaping the makeup of the Legislature. They were no longer passive, even resentful, respondents to what many lobbyists had long regarded as a shakedown in Sacramento. Term limits mean that roughly a third of the Legislature's seats change hands every two years, and that creates genuine contests, especially in primaries, that are not controlled from the Capitol to the previous extent. Declining party identification contributes to the more unpredictable situation in local districts. Thus, while they still direct campaign checks to legislative leaders and key committee chairs, as they had before, new era lobbyists often find themselves traveling around the state interviewing primary candidates, figuring out which ones are most likely to be sympathetic to their clients and, if they look like potential winners, backing them with early money—the kind that makes the biggest impression on legislative hopefuls. By directing money into the campaigns of candidates most likely to support their clients' interests, Capitol lobbyists collectively shift the balance of the Legislature enough to determine the outcome of issues before the gavel has fallen on the first day. Interest groups that do not participate in that form of grassroots politicking can find themselves frozen out, no matter how diligently they may pursue their causes after the Legislature has convened. The California Public

Interest Research Group, a Ralph Nader-inspired reform organization, calculates in a report entitled "Election Inc.," that corporate interests contributed $64.6 million, or about half of the money that went to legislative candidates, in the 2000 election cycle, and those receiving the most corporate money won the vast majority of the contests.

It is, in part, a return to Artie Samish's old "select and elect" system that was shunted aside when strong legislative leaders such as Jesse Unruh and Willie Brown held the reins of power and forced lobbyists to funnel money through them. Lobbyists who are most adept at cultivating candidates early in the biennial process often cash in when their issues hit legislative committees and floors, much to the surprise of their rivals and even legislative leaders. One example is the success of the medical provider lobby in thwarting the drive by personal injury attorneys to raise or eliminate the $250,000 ceiling on pain and suffering damages in malpractice cases. The medical lobbyists used timely campaign contributions and personal contacts to cultivate a coterie of Democrats friendly to their cause while the lawyers operated in the old mode of channeling money to legislative leaders, who were unable to deliver the legislation in a caucus that had been captured by the medical providers before the first trial lawyer bill was introduced.

Inevitably, the breakdown of the old, centralized system of collecting and disbursing money in Sacramento means that lobbyists, and the organizations that employ them, are becoming more involved in the campaign business as they find themselves choosing among primary election hopefuls. They may not pluck someone off skid row, as Artie Samish did, and make him a legislator, but they must assess the degree to which legislative hopefuls are sympathetic to their issues and whether they have a realistic chance of winning. It doesn't help an interest group's postelection access if it backs the losing candidate. As lobbyists and/or managers of an interest group's "political action committee" interview competing candidates they're looking for personal and professional qualities that make them winners, such as a past that's free of crippling blemishes (such as Internal Revenue Service liens or restraining orders from abused spouses), self-confidence to withstand the rigors of a campaign, some record of civic or public service, (local governments have become the most popular springboards to the Legislature in the term limit era), business or professional success, an awareness of the issues that will likely arise in the campaign, at least a minimal level of articulation, a friendly demeanor that's not off-putting to voters, motivation, and an ability to raise a base amount of financial resources, which indicates viability. The interest group gathers intelligence on the district's demographic and political proclivities, gets advice from local leaders in the group's field (prominent realtors if, for example, it's the California Real Estate Association that's making the decision on whom to back), checks preferences of party leaders and assessments of professional campaign managers on the chances of victory. In its more sophisticated forms, the process includes determining which city council or school board member or other local officeholder might be in line for a legislative seat after term limits create a vacancy two or four years in the future and cultivating the potential lawmaker with timely contributions to his or her local campaign. Unwittingly, perhaps, legislative leaders encouraged that aspect of selecting and electing friendly legislators when they drafted Proposition 34, their 2000 ballot measure imposing limits on legislative campaign contributions. They left contributions to local campaigns uncapped, unless they happen to be limited by local laws.

Allen Hoffenblum, a veteran political consultant, has listed five essential factors in a winning legislative campaign: a competitive district, one in which the candidate has at least a theoretical chance to win; a candidate that meets at least minimum personal qualifications; a well-organized and experienced campaign team; a realistic campaign strategy; and, as the bottom line, enough money to carry out the strategy. And how much money is enough? That can vary widely, depending on the district and the circumstances. In a district with a lopsided party registration, where the primary winner is certain to be elected in November and there's little conflict in the primary, as little as $100,000 might do it. But in a highly competitive "swing" district and/or one in which competing factions are battling in the primary—two Latino organizations have been struggling for dominance in Los Angeles, for example—it would not be unusual for an Assembly seat campaign to consume a million dollars, and Senate seats can easily cost several million. Thus, a $5,000 contribution from an interest group can mean a little or a lot, which is why the group's political strategists must be intimately aware of the unique factors at play in any district. Interest groups that have relatively small political warchests have learned to shy away from the big-money races, where their checks would be considered droplets, and concentrate, instead, on cultivating wannabe-legislators in quieter corners of the state, where their money is more appreciated.

The money that flows into the Capitol, or into the campaigns of those seeking to come to the Capitol, is a kind of legal bribery. While straight money-for-votes deals are illegal, and Capitol players insist that money just buys access, it doesn't take a rocket scientist to figure out that a lobbyist who has a generous client is going to fare better than someone who doesn't, and the face-to-face confrontations, such as the one between the Indian tribes and the cardrooms, are proof positive. It's not necessary to be explicit when being implicit works just as well. The master of the indirect transaction is Gray Davis, who, while climbing the political ladder rung by rung developed a reputation as a highly focused political fundraiser. He even confided to a journalist once that the politician he admired the most was former U.S. Senator Alan Cranston because Cranston was willing to pick up the phone and ask for campaign money repeatedly, every day, whether he really wanted to do it or not.

Davis's election to the governorship in 1998 meant that his campaign fundraising went into an even higher gear, and during his first year alone, he packed away some $14 million or some $38,000 a day. By the end of Davis's second year in the Capitol's corner office, his warchest was approaching $27 million. His reputation for being a money-oriented politician meant that special interest groups automatically assumed that they would have to give, and they did, without any particular prodding from the governor or his political aides. Night after night, he would attend receptions at venues around the Capitol, and it was understood that the governor wouldn't grace the event with his presence unless there was at least $100,000 to be collected. He kept up a steady stream of dinners, receptions, luncheons, golf tournaments, and other fundraising events around the state—some of which, such as those thrown by the forest products, health care, and agricultural industries, were staged in conjunction with private discussions by interest group leaders over pending legislation and/or administration policies. "It does give the impression that the governor cares more about fundraising than governing," Jim Knox of Common Cause said at one point, "particularly with some vacancies remaining in the upper levels of the executive branch after a year and a half in office."

Did all of this money buy anyone anything? While the governor's aides insist there were no connections, critics—mostly on the political left—saw pro-industry declarations of policy in such areas as timber harvesting and health maintenance organization regulation follow fundraising meetings between Davis and industry executives. But those in the Capitol shrugged. They saw it simply as the way business is done in California, an inevitable result of the state's wealth and the critical role that state government plays in determining the rules of the game, whether it be how trees are cut down or slot machines are approved. It's money, and it talks.

Will it always be that way? Knox says the lavish fundraising that Davis, other statewide officials, and legislators conduct while deciding important policy questions is "fundamentally corrupt" and other reformers agree. They've tried for years to impose limits on the pay-to-play atmosphere of the Capitol, suggesting specific restrictions on how much individuals and interest groups can donate, how much politicians can spend, and various forms of public financing. And they've been fairly successful in persuading voters to adopt their schemes—although a 2000 version was rejected. Where the reformers have failed is in persuading the courts that their restrictions don't violate constitutional guarantees of free speech in a state where a week's "buy" of statewide television time can easily cost $1 million. In 1996 voters approved Proposition 208, which contained the usual contribution restrictions, and for one year—1997—political fundraising plummeted. But in early 1998, a federal judge voided the measure, saying its limits were too tight to pass free speech muster, and within weeks the Capitol's fundraising machine had cranked up again, eventually reaching epic proportions for the year. The decision may have saved Gray Davis's gubernatorial campaign since he was facing two wealthy rivals in the Democratic primary who could finance their own campaigns and were exempt from Proposition

208's limits. That scare, Davis says, is why he was determined to build up a huge campaign warchest once he had obtained the governorship.

Common Cause and other reform groups have not abandoned the battle. They're still searching for some formula that will attract voters and survive the federal courts. In 2000, as the reformers' 1996-vintage measure, Proposition 208, faced a federal court, legislative leaders made a pre-emptive strike. With Davis's support, the legislators devised—completely in secret—a self-described reform that would impose contribution limits substantially higher than those in Proposition 208, but allow political parties to conduct almost unlimited fundraising and make almost unlimited expenditures for candidates. Reformers branded it a sham aimed at destroying Proposition 208, but it was placed on the 2000 ballot and with a weak opposition campaign, it passed handily. As the measure went into effect in 2001, it soon became clear that it would have little effect. The professionals in the Capitol easily adopted new structures to meet the technical requirements of the measure, and lobbyists continued to arrange for money to flow into the coffers of those considered most friendly to their interests—even if it required some genteel laundering to make it happen.

There is a countervailing theory that imposing the limits the reformers want might make the indirect buying of influence more onerous than it is already. And it goes back to the stakes involved, literally hundreds of billions of dollars each year in budget appropriations, insurance premiums, utility rates, gambling proceeds, and other matters subject to political decision making. The stakes exist and would be unchanged by any campaign contribution limits. Those who want to affect the decisions that politicians make have, therefore, a huge incentive to figure out some way to do it. And if campaign contributions are restricted as an avenue of influence, other, more insidious forms of gaining access and clout will inevitably appear. Perhaps, the only true political reform would be to dismantle the regulatory state itself, thereby reducing the incentive to buy or rent politicians as needed. If the Legislature didn't retain the power to decide who was entitled to an exemption from the "tied house" liquor laws, or if it didn't determine which breed of horse could race on which day, or what kind of gambling casino could offer which form of gaming, there wouldn't be as great a need to influence what it did.

CHAPTER 5

The Politics of Personal Relationships

The Legislature is dependent on lobbyists for information, as God in-
tended it to be—An anonymous lobbyist, said to be drunk at the time,
quoted in former Senator James Mills's book A Disorderly House

The high-ranking adviser to California's governor had a problem—a simultane-
ous involvement with two women with neither being aware of his affair with the
other. But the personal politics of the dilemma, a staple of Hollywood scriptwrit-
ing, were compounded by the intrusion of Capitol politics because the women in
his life were lobbyists working the opposing sides of a high-profile legislative
issue.

   The bill, dealing with an arcane facet of medical care, involved millions of
dollars for their rival clients, and to each lobbyist it was the high point of her
professional career, one that demanded full-time attention and the deployment of
all tactical weapons at her command. That included perhaps, a personal relationship with a high-ranking gubernatorial aide on whose desk the bill could land if
it passed the Legislature and went to the governor for a signature or veto. Each
woman would press her client's case, each would know that his advice to the
governor might play a critical role. And whatever the final outcome, his love life
would become even more complicated than it already was.

   As it turned out, the juggler of women was saved by fate. The lobbyist
working against the bill was more skillful, or luckier, than her rival, and the
measure died in the legislative process without reaching the governor. But his
dilemma illustrates, in somewhat farcical terms, the complicated, interdependent
relationship between lobbyists and Capitol politicians.

Contemporary life is filled with symbiotic relationships, mutual dependence mixed with wariness, skepticism, and even hostility. After all, if society wasn't plagued by criminals, it wouldn't need police officers, prosecutors, defense attorneys, criminal trial judges, probation officers, jailers, bail bondsmen, burglar alarm services, prison builders, or handcuff manufacturers, to name but a few occupations whose livelihoods depend on the human tendency to steal or commit violence.

Symbiosis is a simple fact of life in the Capitol, a village existing in the middle of a medium-sized California city, containing the elements of any small town overlaid with the peculiarities of a high-stakes political poker game. Relationships in the Capitol are essentially personal, rather than institutional or even rational, and at the heart of its daily life are the relationships between 120 legislators and 10 times as many lobbyists who represent thousands of clients trying to affect what those lawmakers—as well as the governor and his aides—do in their official capacities. The politicians need the lobbyists and the lobbyists need the politicians, and that mutual dependence, often friendly, even affectionate, but at times tinged with suspicion and envy, creates public policy for 35 million Californians.

In the broadest terms, there are three levels of symbiosis in the Capitol, although they are constantly intermingled, and it's never easy to determine where one ends and another begins. One is legislative—lobbyists provide information, feedback, outside support, and negotiating skills in partnership with legislators to accomplish what both desire. Another is purely political—lobbyists provide money and organizational support to help friendly politicians get elected and re-elected, hoping it will improve their chances of winning legislative battles, and the politicians make implicit, if not explicit, promises of cooperation if their needs are met.

But when the going gets tough, the third level of relationship, the personal, often carries the day. Friendships are forged in hours of togetherness at dinners, bouts of bar-hopping, golf tournaments, and fishing trips and manifest themselves in the altogether human desire to help one's friends affect the outcome of legislation. These personal relationships take on an added fillip when the legislator and the lobbyist are of opposite genders, a situation that has become much more common with the increases in female legislators and lobbyists. That there have been numerous affairs between lobbyists and politicians is undeniable, but whether they involved political motives or merely hormonal ones is never certain. There was, for instance, a state senator who was "dating" a lobbyist for major corporation while simultaneously carrying legislation that was eventually signed into law and meant millions of dollars for the lobbyist's employer. The two lovebirds went on one tropical vacation paid by the corporation but the senator insisted that his liaison with the lobbyist was not a factor in the legislation, calling it "a bona fide dating relationship," parroting the language of a state regulation that carves out an exception to the restrictions on exchanges between legislators and lobbyists. Another senator carried on a decades-long relationship with a lobbyist who was his former aide. The two were accepted in Sacramento as a couple although he and his wife were a couple in southern California. The lobbyist/girlfriend represented some local government clients in the senator's district, for whom he often carried legislation. A woman lobbyist for one governor was famous for pressing her ample bosom into the arm of a legislator as she earnestly pleaded with him to vote with the governor. And when employees of Continental Airlines descended on the Capitol to plead for legislation that would allow them to buy the company, many of the flight attendants went carousing with legislators, giving rise to a joke: "What's a Continental sandwich? One legislator and two stewardesses."

While these and other examples fuel the debate over women in lobbying, the vast majority of women in the field operate professionally and avoid situations that might set tongues to wagging in the gossip-prone Capitol. And the chaste women lobbyists seethe when the activities of other women—such as the flashy blonde who breaks out her low-cut, see-through blouses when close votes are pending—contribute to the notion that sex sells in the Capitol. By the end of the century, a new current had developed in the stream of Capitol gossip about personal relations between lobbyists and legislators. As the ranks of women in the Legislature swelled from a handful to dozens in the 1990s, some male lobbyists acquired reputations for using their masculine charms to persuade certain female lawmakers of the validity of their arguments. One middle-aged female senator was said to be particularly susceptible to the blandishments of young male lobbyists dispatched by their firms to argue their clients' cases—much to the despair of others trying to catch the senator's ear.

The modern history of the Legislature is largely one of the evolving relationship between those who make public policy decisions and those who want to affect those decisions. And no one understood the interplay between personal and political better than Artie Samish, who virtually invented many of the lobbying techniques still in use today and applied them from a suite in the Senator Hotel, across from the Capitol on L Street.

"Sometimes I would get up at seven to breakfast with a senator before he went to the Capitol," Samish wrote in his revealing autobiography, *The Secret Boss of California*. "By eight, some of the committees were already holding their meetings and some of the telephones started ringing with reports from my Gestapo (Capitol aides whom Samish paid to keep him informed. . . .

"Throughout the day I received visitors both big and small: legislators and state executives, brewery owners and bartenders, newspaper publishers and bootblacks. All received the same Samish hospitality. A buffet served lobster, shrimp, caviar, and other goodies. I ran the best-stocked bar in Sacramento. And neither I nor my two chief aides. Frank Flynn and Bill Jasper, ever took a drink."

Samish recounted how a bill for one of his clients was in danger of being rejected because a couple of legislators whose votes were critical had skipped out of the Capitol. "They had taken a couple of girls on a voyage of the Delta Queen, the steamboat that made an overnight trip between Sacramento and San Francisco," Samish wrote, saying that he was able to determine what stops the paddlewheel steamer would make along the way and used his influence to get a couple of Highway Patrol officers to intercept the craft and haul the two errant legislators back to Sacramento with sirens blaring. After they had voted as Samish wanted, he had an aide drive them to San Francisco before the Delta Queen arrived. "I'd hate to have those two girls arrive with no one to greet them." (The Delta King, the Delta Queen's sister ship, is now permanently docked on the Sacramento riverfront as a hotel and is the frequent site of political fundraising events, as well as the occasional tryst.)

Samish's book is loaded with stories of how he tended his legislative flock, from getting lawmakers elected in the first place to seeing to their entertainment in Sacramento and making sure that they received enough outside income to feel comfortable about being legislators for a few hundred dollars a year. And all they had to do in return was vote for his clients' interests, mostly in establishing and maintaining state-enforced monopolies in liquor and other lucrative trades.

If Samish's attitude was that legislators didn't need to know anything about his clients' bills other than what he told them, it was not much different from those of mid-20th century governors. The Legislature in those days had only a few clerical employees and was utterly dependent on lobbyists and administration officials for information about the impact of legislation, although after World War II the Legislature did establish its first budget analysis office. The big change in that relationship came with the rise of Jesse Unruh as a legislative power in the late 1950s. Unruh made it his life's work to create a Legislature that was independent of lobbyists and administration officials in terms of information and partially independent of lobbyists in political terms as well, even if he was every bit as much a party animal as his predecessors, an enthusiastic participant in the carousing that has always been an after-hours feature of life in the Capitol. Unruh signaled his pursuit of legislative independence when, as Assembly Ways and Means Committee chairman, he hired a budget staff adviser and irritated Governor Pat Brown, who considered it an insult that his Department of Finance would no longer be the Legislature's primary source of fiscal information. "Unruh was declaring his independence of the governor and the third house at the same time," a legislative lieutenant, James Mills, later wrote in his memoirs of the Unruh era, *A Disorderly House.*

Once he had won the speakership in 1961, Unruh expanded the concept, adding hundreds of bodies to the Capitol staff, in theory to give the Legislature untainted, objective advice about legislation that, then as now, mostly originates outside the building with state agencies or lobbyists for the myriad interest groups. Unruh made certain that the minority Republicans had a share of the staff, albeit not as large a one as Democrats enjoyed. Simultaneously, Unruh began centralizing the campaign fundraising process, insisting that lobbyists direct a larger share of their money through him or trusted lieutenants, and arguing that such a process would insulate lawmakers from *quid pro quo* arrangements. That it had the ancillary effect of bolstering Unruh's power over his members was dismissed as incidental to the main goal of making the Legislature more independent.

Initially, Unruh's reforms appeared to work marvelously, resulting in a steady flow of creative legislation on civil rights, consumer protection, and environmental conservation. So impressed were academics that the California Legislature became the national model of how a state legislative body should work. But in creating these new regulatory schemes, supposedly to bring more egalitarianism to California, Unruh was also creating more business for lobbyists—more incentive, as it were, to improve their relationships with legislators. In the end, that motive penetrated the insulating blanket that Unruh created.

Unruh never discouraged the personal side of the lobbyist-legislator relationship. As legislators became full-timers, they spent more time in Sacramento and less in their districts and the Capitol developed a schedule that is still largely in effect. During the early days of the Unruh regime, Southern California legislators would leave Los Angeles by train on Sunday night, drink and play cards during the overnight trip, and show up in Sacramento Monday morning. Monday, Tuesday and Wednesday nights were times for carousing and everyone departed on Thursday, which is known in the Capitol as "getaway day." The train riders would spend another night on the rails and arrive back in Los Angeles Friday morning. Later, when airline service became more frequent, legislators would fly in on Monday morning and fly out on Thursday, still leaving three nights for fun and games. The schedule is designed to take maximum advantage of a self-serving provision of state law that allows legislators to claim "per diem," more than $100 a day, tax-free, seven days a week as long as they're not out of session more than three consecutive days. It explains why the Legislature conducts brief sessions, some of which consist of nothing more than legislators signing their names to "check in" sheets, on Fridays when Mondays are part of three-day holidays. They're known to Capitol insiders as "per diem sessions" that keep the expense checks flowing.

As the Legislature went into full-time mode, some lawmakers moved their families to Sacramento—risking, in some cases, allegations that they were abandoning their districts—while others simply didn't care for the nightly carousing. But for many, life in Sacramento became an almost collegiate experience as they spent their days working and their nights partying, with Unruh often leading the carousers. Mills's *A Disorderly House* recites numerous incidents in which the speaker and his entourage would move from bar to bar in their quest of good times. And lobbyists knew—at least for a couple of decades—that nothing solidifies a relationship more than getting drunk together, particularly when the lobbyists were picking up the restaurant and bar tabs. Indeed, some powerful legislators could simply sign the names of lobbyists to their tabs in restaurants and bars around the Capitol and expect them to be paid.

Samish and his lavish Senator Hotel buffet vanished, but countless other lobbyists filled the vacuum with their own versions of his largesse. Some staged annual dinners or weekly lunches where legislators could eat and drink their fill. The railroad lobby called its Thursday lunch the "caboose" while health care lobbyists termed their Wednesday lunch "clam and coral." One of the more famous lobbyist-sponsored luncheon clubs was "Moose Milk," sponsored by liquor distributors, while local governments played the game with an every-Monday event at the Sutter Club, then an all-male bastion of good food, well-aged liquors, and cigars just two blocks from the Capitol. Today, it is much the same thing, except for its admission of women. The most revered of these noon-time institutions was the Derby Club, originally formed by state Senator Randolph Collier, who almost single-handedly created California's extensive system of freeways after World War II as chairman of the Senate Transportation Committee, which explains why if Collier created the Derby Club, the road contractors, oil companies, and building materials suppliers who constituted the "highway lobby" financed it.

Legend has it that Collier, who was first elected to the Legislature in 1938 and served until the late 1970s, was walking down New York's Fifth Avenue with several colleagues and highway lobbyists in 1957 when he saw the fashionably dressed men and women and, on a whim, popped into a clothing store, where every member of his party acquired a derby hat and an umbrella. They were so impressed with their natty appearance that they decided to wear the hats to a weekly luncheon in Sacramento, convened at Posey's, a restaurant near the Capitol popular with legislators and lobbyists. The original membership was 13 and it became a virtual fraternity, with new members coming in by invitation only and being subjected to secret admission votes. Eventually, about 150 lobbyists and legislators belonged and the unwritten terms of admission were acceptance of the mutually dependent and mutually profitable relationship between legislators and lobbyists for special interest clients.

Like those of any fraternity, whether of the collegiate variety or such groups as the Masonic Lodge, members depended on each other. A Derby Club lobbyist or legislator could call on a fraternity brother for a timely vote, a timely campaign contribution, or some political lubricating oil, giving members an important edge when dealing with nonmembers. Membership carried fringe benefits, such as top professional entertainment from Hollywood or New York at the weekly luncheons, black tie dinners, and, on occasion, raunchy entertainment of the stag party variety. Public officials from all levels, up to the governor, were invited to some Derby Club events, and during the 1960s and early 1970s its members were the Capitol's power elite.

As the Derby Club became a symbol of Capitol power, it also became a target for political reformers, to whom it embodied everything that was wrong about the system. Jerry Brown knew first-hand about the social side of Capitol life from his father's governorship, and when he ran for governor himself in 1974, he seized upon the public's Watergate-spawned revulsion against sleazy politics by sponsoring a ballot measure, the Political Reform Act, aimed at the heart of the Derby Club by imposing strict limits on what lobbyists could spend on entertaining legislators. There was even some talk about disbanding what had become a Capitol institution. But it survived, at least for a while, with legislators paying for their own lunches. It even admitted women in the early 1980s, which meant that the stag party aspects of its meetings were cleaned up. Capitol old-timers just liked getting together with their friends, regardless of whether it involved legislation or politics, as illustrated by one incident from the 1980s. At the first Derby Club meeting of the year, the presiding officer, then-Senator Al Alquist of San Jose, imposed a tongue-in-cheek fine on long-time liquor and horseracing lobbyist James Garibaldi for "getting married without my permission" during the Legislature's off-season. Another lobbyist, former Assemblyman Frank Murphy, jumped up and offered to pay the fine, generating a raucous laugh from attendees. Not only was Murphy a close friend of Garibaldi, but The Judge's new wife was Murphy's ex-wife and the wedding saved Murphy several thousand dollars a month in alimony.

The Derby Club is no longer a symbol of insider power in the Capitol, but its decline doesn't mean that social relationships aren't carefully cultivated by lobbyists looking for that all-important edge in the game of passing and defeating legislation important to their clients. And for decades, the venue of choice for improving those relationships was Frank Fat's restaurant, two blocks from the Capitol down L Street and just around the corner from the Sutter Club. The story of Fat's, as Capitol insiders call the long, narrow restaurant, is quintessential California, about a teenager who made his way to Sacramento from China in 1919, slept under a sidewalk near the railroad station and finally found a job in a small Chinese restaurant owned by his cousin. Frank Fat learned the restaurant business, returned to China briefly to get married and start a family, and with the $2,000 he had carefully saved, opened his own eatery on L Street in 1939, in a former "bootlegger joint" in what was then a very tough corner of the city.

"L Street used to be a very poor street," Fat recalled in a newspaper interview, not long before his 1997 death at age 92. "Nobody walked on L Street. All my friends said I'm crazy. They think it's a very poor location. They said even a dog wouldn't go there."

What was unsuitable for dogs became, after a time, very suitable for Capitol politicians, who liked the ambiance and proximity of Fat's. At least a dozen governors dined at the restaurant at one time or another, along with countless legislators, lobbyists, and visiting celebrities. In the 1980s, it was extensively refurbished with an art deco theme, but the bar remained the restaurant's most dominant feature, pepper steak and banana cream pie remained its most popular items, and a tiny upstairs room still hosted private luncheons, dinners, and the occasional high-stakes poker game. After Frank Fat died, his politically savvy son, Wing Fat, continued to greet patrons at the door and preside over a small empire of restaurants bearing the family's distinctive name.

How many political deals have been consummated at Fat's? No one knows, although they have to number in the thousands, the most famous of which was the many-sided "napkin deal" of 1987 that rewrote the state's rules on personal liability lawsuits. Beyond the deals, Fat's evolved into a kind of private club for lobbyists and legislators, reaching its peak in the 1980s and early 1990s, in part due to the patronage of the Capitol's most powerful figure of the era, Assembly Speaker Willie Brown. Later in the decade, after Brown departed to become mayor of San Francisco and several of Fat's steadiest patrons died, the restaurant's preeminent position eroded. A couple of newer restaurants, closer to the Capitol and new office buildings housing lobbyists, offered strong competition for the political dollar, even if the old-timers continued to patronize Fat's. And one bistro, Brannan's, just across from the Capitol on L Street, advertises its role as an adjunct site of politicking by decorating its walls with rare political posters and keeping its television sets tuned to floor and committee sessions, much as sports bars cater to sports fans. More than one lobbyist or legislator has sat at Brannan's huge bar, kept an eye on proceedings via TV, and dashed across the street when his or her issue was coming to a vote.

Simon's, a Chinese restaurant and bar a couple of blocks east of the Capitol, became a popular hangout in the 1990s—something of a throwback to the earlier days of Frank Fat's—after a prominent Senate leader, Bill Lockyer, made it his unofficial headquarters simply because he lived in a nearby apartment house. Even after Lockyer left the Senate (where he was president pro tem) and became attorney general, legislators from both parties continued to congregate at Simon's. "Politicians need a place like this," owner Simon Chan told a reporter. "People feel at home here. They can be casual and comfortable and walk in here in a T-shirt and mingle with friends." A regular patron, Los Angeles Assemblyman Herb Wesson described Simon's as being "like Cheers, where everybody knows your name." And lobbyists quickly learned that Simon's was a place to patronize if one wanted to make private deals on legislation—or simply keep track of what was happening.

As legislative campaign fundraising became centralized in Sacramento during the 1980s, legislators and even hopefuls began staging hundreds of breakfasts, luncheons, receptions, and, occasionally, dinners to attract dollars from lobbyists and their clients, although the lavish tribute dinners were more likely to be held in legislators' hometowns. Regardless of the locale, legislators are implicitly selling access to themselves and colleagues to those willing to buy tickets, often costing $1,000 or more, making these "fundraising events," as they're termed, both social and financial occasions. Often, legislators and lobbyists who see each other during the work day in Sacramento will board the same airliners to fly to Los Angeles for a fundraising dinner in the evening and then fly back together the next morning to resume work in the Capitol. Legislators may be less interested in who showed up at their events then who bought tickets, but lobbyists often conclude that as long as they or their clients are paying the price, they may as well use the opportunity to improve personal relationships.

These opportunities became more important after the advent of term limits in the 1990s because, unlike their predecessors, term-limited lawmakers are less likely to come from legislative staffs and have established relationships with lobbyists. Keeping track of who's up and who's down in a Legislature with a high turnover is more difficult for lobbyists, and fundraising events, often lubricated with alcohol, can be an important intelligence-gathering venue. The fundraising events themselves became more elaborate during the 1990s, often involving golf tournaments at fancy resorts or deep-sea fishing excursions, complete with commemorative hats or polo shirts—and higher ticket prices, of course.

A variation on the theme is what one might call a migration of the political herd. Political conventions, both state and national, often attract packs of Sacramento lobbyists, who seek not only intelligence about present and future political conditions, but opportunities to schmooze with lawmakers in different venues. Special interest groups often "sponsor" various convention activities to cement relations with party leaders—Indian tribes being particularly active in that arena. During the 1996 Democratic National Convention in Chicago, for example, California delegates—many of them legislators—had to sit through lengthy expositions on Indian history as the price of having their expenses underwritten by one casino-owning tribe.

Another migration is the annual spring visit that legislative leaders of both parties—and dozens of carefully selected lieutenants—pay to Washington, ostensibly to lobby Congress and federal agencies on behalf of California interests. There are two or three Sacramento lobbyists for every legislator, and their clients spend hundreds of thousands of dollars not only for traveling expenses but lavish social and entertainment events each evening. By having interest groups pick up the tabs directly, rather than doing it themselves, lobbyists can skirt the Political Reform Act's limits on entertaining legislators. The annual Washington trip gets larger and more elaborate each year—the 2000 version was financed by a $165,000 fund created by $2,500 donations from 66 corporations and business groups, plus tens of thousands of dollars paid by individual interest groups for specific social events. There were so many expensive cigars fired up in the Mayflower Hotel hospitality suite maintained by the business sponsors that the smoke set off a fire alarm at 1 a.m., sending 500 guests into the night.

Socializing at fundraising events, conventions, and the Washington trip has two effects on what emerges from the legislative mill. It gives those who buy tickets and attend additional access to lawmakers and an edge over those who don't buy into the system, either because of a lack of money or internal policies. Some of the nation's largest corporations, for example, refuse to make state-level campaign contributions, putting extra pressure on their lobbyists. The social whirl also creates pressure on others to play the game, fearing that their rivals in legislative wars will get an important edge if they buy tickets and attend events.

The relationship between lobbyists and legislators, however, is more complex than simply exchanging time for money. When it comes to passing or defeating legislation, they may become virtual partners. While the lobbyist may look to the legislator to carry the bill, or lead opposition, the lawmaker looks to the lobbyist for logistical support, such as generating support from constituent or special interest groups, doping out the opposition, negotiating with interest groups on amendments, or lining up witnesses for hearings. Except for money, the relationship is pretty much the same whether the lobbyist's client is a wealthy trade group, a government agency, or a nonprofit public interest group. The lobbyist's job is to win on the issue, however he or she can, within the strictures of the law.

Two episodes involving one of the co-authors, when he was a representative of the University of California system in the 1970s, illustrate how even a governmental lobbyist must lubricate relationships with powerful legislators.

Both incidents had to do with the University of California's overriding interest in maintaining close relations with the two legislators who at that time held life-and-death power over the university's all-important annual budget allocation, Senate Finance Committee chairman Randolph Collier and Assembly Ways and Means Committee chairman Willie Brown. Until a big procedural change in the mid-1970s, which occurred for reasons that will later become evident, these two chairmen wrote the final version of the state budget themselves, without public hearings, and were virtually the sole arbiters of which agency or program got what amount of money.

At the time, the Ways and Means Committee had the dual responsibility to oversee the budget and act as a funnel or traffic cop for all major legislation. With the chairman's enormous clout, he was courted by every lobbyist in the Capitol. In late 1972 or early 1973, Brown contacted the UC lobbyist and told him it was "imperative" that a young San Francisco constituent be admitted to the UC San Francisco Medical School, the applicant being the son of a close friend of Brown's, a San Francisco civic leader and newspaper publisher. The lobbyist, mindful that his employer had an $800 million per year stake in the state budget Brown commanded, responded tactfully that "every consideration will be given" to the young man's application. "You are not hearing me," Brown replied after a short pause. "I don't want him to receive every consideration. I want him admitted." And with that, Brown hung up the phone.

The UC lobbyist, knowing he had a delicate situation dropped into his lap, quickly contacted the UCSF admissions office and learned that the medical-wannabe's qualifications were good, but not quite up to the level of other applicants and that he had not completed three required premed undergraduate courses. The young man qualified for the university's affirmative action admissions program due to his ethnicity, but his application had been denied in favor of other minority applicants because he displayed "inadequate motivation" in the eyes of admissions officials and "lack of interest in completing prerequisite courses." Notations about "arrogance" and "attitude" also made his admission to the medical school on his merits unlikely, even though three-quarters of the "special admissions" panel shared the lad's ethnic background.

The UC lobbyist advised top UCSF administrators of the political problem posed by Brown's imperious demand, noting that the Ways and Means chairman was not accustomed to having his wishes thwarted and that he might well signal displeasure with a negative UC response by slashing its budget appropriation. And rejecting his son would alienate someone who published a newspaper with wide circulation among minority readers. The issue was kicked upstairs to the medical school's chancellor, a distinguished physician and educator who had previously demonstrated courage under political fire. The chancellor mulled over the situation and agreed to admit the young man if he completed the required premed courses. He also pledged to personally counsel the student in the "value of humility" and "respect for egalitarian principles."

The UC lobbyist hurriedly arranged a private meeting with Brown to convey the good news, but quickly learned that the chairman didn't see it the same way. Bristling at the chancellor's conditions, Brown told the lobbyist, "You go back and tell those bastards that if this kid is not admitted forthwith, without any conditions, the university's 1973–74 budget will be reduced by $10 million." That ultimatum was quickly delivered to the lobbyist's masters and the big cheese himself, the president of the entire UC system, entered the fray. After hearing of Brown's demands and taking cryptic notes, the president told the lobbyist, "You know, a $10 million loss will do less damage to this institution than establishing a precedent which will place us on the slippery slope to mediocrity. If it is acceptable to the chancellor (of UCSF), tell the chairman that we will waive the one undergraduate course which has little to do with studying medicine, but we can't admit a student who is ill-prepared to grasp the core curriculum of medical school and we can't waive the other two pre-med courses. Do what you can to mitigate the loss but if we have to take it, we will."

The chancellor agreed and Brown was informed of the new offer, rejecting it as quickly as he had the previous conditions. The student was not admitted to the medical school, and three weeks later, the Assembly's version of the budget emerged from the Ways and Means Committee with a $10 million reduction from what its subcommittees had recommended for the UC subsidy from the state.

Eventually, the tale of the $10 million cut was conveyed to Ronald Reagan, the governor of California, who laughed and jokingly told the UC lobbyist that "If you can guarantee admission to medical school for a son of a friend of mine, I will make sure the $10 million cut is restored." Actually, the money was restored at the insistence of state senators, over Brown's objections. And the following year, after completing the required undergraduate courses, the young man who started the entire affair was admitted to the UC medical school. He later became a practicing physician.

The UC lobbyist's involvement with Randy Collier was more political than personal, but also involved, at least on the periphery, Willie Brown. It stemmed from a political impasse between Republican Reagan and the Democrat-controlled Legislature over the redrawing of legislative districts after the 1970 census. Reagan had refused to sign redistricting plans drawn up by the Democrats for the simple reason that they would have locked in Democratic control of the Capitol. The impasse led to a shift of the redistricting issue to the state Supreme Court, which had its own set of maps drawn up and implemented.

Collier, who represented the northwestern corner of California including Siskiyou and Del Norte counties, was known as "The Silver Fox of the Siskiyous" and "Father of the California Freeway System," the latter from his long chairmanship of the Senate Transportation Committee after World War II when new highways were built at a furious pace. Eventually, Collier traded the transportation chair for the Senate Finance Committee, which played the same role in the Senate that Ways and Means did in the Assembly.

The court-ordered redistricting plan gave Collier a new district that he didn't particularly want, one that stretched down the North Coast of California and forced him to deal with hundreds of thousands of new constituents. Concerned about winning re-election in the new district, Collier decided to use his power over the state budget to impress his new constituents with his ability to deliver the goodies from Sacramento, a flock of new park projects and some appropriations to assist the region's chronically depressed economy.

The UC lobbyist was unaware of the larger strategy when, one day in 1974, he was asked to accompany Collier on a trip to the North Coast to visit a politically influential businessman named Bill Grader. Grader, once the top aide to the region's Democratic congressman, had run for Congress himself in 1963 after his boss was killed in a plane crash, only to lose to a little-known Republican in a special election. Grader owned a restaurant in Bodega Bay but was known mostly as the political voice of the region's commercial fishermen. The specific destination for the UC lobbyist and Collier that day was an aquaculture program that the University of California was running in Bodega Bay, researching whether new forms of seafood—lobsters specifically—could be successfully cultivated and commercially exploited.

Collier drove the lobbyist to Bodega Bay from Sacramento in his powder-blue, state-supplied Lincoln, often hitting speeds of 90 miles an hour on the twisting backcountry roads, and arrived at Grader's restaurant at 10:30 a.m. Collier ordered a quart of vodka and a supply or orange juice and the visitors began drinking. After three quarts of vodka had been consumed—all on the UC expense account—the party, including Grader, went to the UC aquaculture facility for a tour, which was conducted with great solicitousness by the university researchers.

On the return trip to Sacramento, Collier asked the UC lobbyist what he thought about the university's ending its direct operation of the program and contracting it out to someone else. The lobbyist reacted somewhat negatively, explaining that the research on lobsters had been inconclusive, as well as expensive, but Collier, the lobbyist could see, was adamant. And two months later, when the state budget emerged from committee, there was a provision that transferred the aquaculture research program from UC to the state, along with a slice of the UC budget to finance it, and a requirement that the research be contracted out to someone else.

The UC lobbyist was stunned and, inquiring about how the transfer had occurred, learned that it was only one of a series of provisions stuck into the budget bill by Collier—with Willie Brown's assistance—all of which related to the new district in which Collier would be seeking re-election. The lobbyist became involved in the developing opposition to the Collier pork barrel grab, along with the Legislature's highly respected budget analyst, A. Alan Post, and Senator Tony Beilensen. Post's role was a bit dicey, since he tried to avoid the internal politics of the Capitol and in aiding the opposition, he risked alienating a very powerful legislator in Collier. Post drew up a list of several dozen questionable pork barrel projects and delivered it, in a plain envelope, to the UC lobbyist, who passed it on to Beilensen and other senators who were looking for ammunition that would stall the Collier-Brown budget, written by the two in secret and presented to the Legislature as a *fait accompli*. The list of what came to be known as "park barrel" projects angered the senators serving on the Finance Committee because they had previously rejected most of them and considered Collier's actions to be a breach of legislative protocol. And Collier's rural conservatism—he was a Republican in everything but registration—grated on urban liberals who welcomed a chance to loosen his grip on the budget.

After Collier presented his version of the budget to the full Senate, Beilensen arose and began reading from the list of projects that Collier had inserted. The anger among other senators increased as he went down the list. The budget was defeated, a new budget conference committee was appointed, and Collier was stripped of his Finance Committee chairmanship by Senate President Pro Tem Jim Mills—who delivered the bad news to Collier in the tiny bathroom off Mills's Capitol office. Beilensen replaced Collier at the helm of Finance, and Collier resumed the chairmanship of the Transportation Committee. He left the Legislature—to which he was first elected in 1938—a few years later. Thereafter, budget conference committees were open, but the budget-writing process largely returned to the back rooms in the 1990s and the kind of pork-grabbing that got Collier into trouble in the 1970s became commonplace.

CHAPTER 6

Organizing Grassroots, or Is It Astroturf?

When I feel the heat, I see the light—Everett Dirksen, U.S. Senate Republican leader during the 1960s

Dugald Gillies didn't invent grassroots organization as the vital third leg in an effective program of influencing political decision making in Sacramento, but as the chief lobbyist for the California Real Estate Association (CREA) in the 1970s and 1980s, he demonstrated its power as few have done before or since. Real estate agents are, by their nature, outgoing and aggressive, and pounding the hallways of the Capitol and engaging legislators in conversation is not too much different from persuading buyers and sellers of homes to come to terms.

Residential real estate was in flux during the period that Gillies represented its interests in Sacramento. California's once-soaring population growth slowed markedly in the 1970s, reducing the chief generator of home sales. During the latter part of the decade, soaring interest rates threatened to bring the market to a screeching halt, along with the commission-based incomes of Gillies' clients.

Gillies had already demonstrated the power of grassroots lobbying with his ability, virtually at a moment's notice, to flood the Capitol with hundreds of real estate agents in pastel blazers. Coupled with the industry's regular campaign contributions to key legislators and Gillies' own intimate knowledge of his issues and the Legislature, the CREA's grassroots campaign made it a formidable foe in any political battle—a classic example of the "three-legged stool" that has become the model approach to influence the California Legislature. All of those tools would come into play as Gillies faced a showdown with a rival whose in-

93

fluence in the Legislature was legendary: the mortgage loan industry, both banks and savings and loan institutions in the days when they were distinct entities.

Banks—including such California-born giants as Bank of America and Wells Fargo—had strong, decades-long connections to the Republican party while the savings and loans were equally well-connected to Democrats. An icon of California political lore is that the S&Ls, shunned by the bankers and their Republican allies after World War II, turned to Democrats as a source of political support and especially to Jesse Unruh, a rising young Los Angeles politician. Unruh, it's been said, was a virtual creation of S&L pioneer Howard Ahmanson (whose son, ironically, became a financier of conservative causes decades later). The tradition continued into the 1970s and 1980s, until financial deregulation virtually ended distinctions between banks and S&Ls and when the two worked together on a banking-related political issue, the coalition was generally overpowering.

Just such an issue arose in the late 1970s as interest rates spiked to the dizzying 20 percent level and real estate brokers resorted to "creative financing" to keep their trade alive. Buyers were unwilling to take out new mortgages at the higher rates, so agents encouraged them to assume the lower-interest mortgages that homeowners already possessed and pay sellers the difference in either cash or through second mortgages held by the sellers.

Bankers and savings and loan executives despised the deals they couldn't hike the interest rate on the new owners by writing a new mortgage. "Creative financing" also kept them from offsetting the higher interest rates they were paying and eliminating low-profit existing mortgages. It was the political equivalent of the unstoppable force—real estate agents' will to survive—and the immovable object—the powerful banking industry.

The key issue was whether new buyers could assume home mortgages without an upgrade in interest rates. The bankers rolled out their heavy guns to press the Legislature to either outlaw assumable mortgages or allow the banks to raise their interest rates. Their measure was rolling through the Capitol until Gillies and his real estate brokers began hammering legislators with their message that doing what the lenders wanted would effectively preclude their constituents from buying and selling their homes and would ignite a firestorm should voters learn how the legislators voted. The showdown came when Gillies, appearing alone against a phalanx of dark-suited bankers at one committee hearing, reminded its members again of the political peril they faced—the wrath of home sellers and buyers—by doing the lenders' bidding. Support for the bill collapsed as Gillies spoke and the vote was postponed—forever, as it turned out. Years later, lobbyists still were talking about how Gillies had stared down the bankers and won, crediting his personal standing and the demonstrated energy of his grassroots foot soldiers for the win.

Grassroots organization is an important adjunct of lobbying because Californians pay only scant attention to politics. Californians' mobility, their shallow allegiance to any community, and their lackadaisical attitude toward voting are components of that syndrome, one that early 20th-century political reformers inadvertently encouraged by reducing the power of political parties and making local governments nonpartisan. Only in a few communities—San Francisco being the most prominent—does political interest and participation reach the levels common to eastern states.

Grassroots organization is aimed at stirring up activity—phone calls, letters, email, faxes, newspaper editorials, personal visits—to pressure politicians on behalf of a particular cause by demonstrating how the issue affects the interests of constituents and voters. Capitol politicians may be shielded by layers of aides and made-to-order districts, but all other factors considered equal, they'd rather not offend significant numbers of their own constituents, especially in an era of term limits, when one might be seeking another office soon.

Lobbyists debate among themselves whether grassroots pressure is more important than campaign money in bending legislators, and the consensus is that it depends on the situation. All other factors being equal, most politicians also would prefer not to offend major campaign donors. The two working together—backed by a professional lobbying staff—are almost unstoppable. Occasionally, however, the two factors are at cross-purposes. One side of the issue may have the money and little or no grassroots support while the other may have no money but a lot of bodies. In that scenario, other factors—such as media interest—may come into play but if it's money vs. grassroots, the latter probably will prevail.

Candy Lightner, a Sacramento single mother, drove home that point in the early 1980s when, almost single-handedly, she changed the political climate regarding drunken driving, defeating not only powerful liquor industry forces but a hostile Capitol culture. Lightner created Mothers Against Drunk Driving (MADD) after her teen-age daughter was killed by an intoxicated motorist. Until Lightner organized mothers of drunken driving victims and began pestering lawmakers, they had tended to treat the matter lightly. Drinking, sometimes to excess, was a popular after-hours activity among Capitol denizens, and several legislators had been nailed for drunken driving themselves. But after Lightner's campaign captured media and public attention, the Legislature passed a series of laws lowering the legal limits on drivers' blood alcohol levels and increasing the penalties. MADD moved on to become a nationwide movement, shifting its headquarters to Texas, and Lightner's cultural status was affirmed by her becoming the subject of a made-for-television movie. Ironically, she was later forced out of MADD by a power struggle.

As Lightner demonstrated, the most valuable asset for a shoestring operation is to have a cause that naturally creates interest in the media and the public. When, for example, Fresno photographer Mike Reynolds launched his one-man crusade in the early 1990s to pass a "three-strikes-and-you're out" sentencing law to crack down on repeat offenders, even his own tragic story, the murder of his daughter in conjunction with a street robbery, didn't move the Legislature. Liberal Democrats who didn't—and still don't—like the idea of giving long sentences to two- and three-time offenders even for relatively minor crimes buried Reynolds' bill in the Assembly. But when a 13-year-old girl named Polly Klaas was abducted from her Petaluma home and brutally murdered by an unrepentant felon who had just been released from prison, Reynolds' tough-on-crime measure suddenly was catapulted onto the front pages and with some critical money from the state prison guards union, quickly qualified for the statewide ballot. The Assembly just as quickly reversed itself and passed the law itself.

Grassroots organization became a more important factor in Capitol lobbying during the 1990s because the advent of term limits brought into the Capitol fewer professional politicians and more graduates of local civic organizations and local governments, who were more attuned to local attitudes and less connected to Sacramento's professional lobbyists. It was inevitable that specialists in organizational work would evolve, some on the staffs of major trade and professional organizations, working hand-in-hand with lobbyists, and some in "public relations" firms that expanded in both number and size during the decade. By decade's end, it was increasingly unclear where the line was to be drawn between public relations and lobbying, the two trades having become so closely intertwined.

Without a cause that naturally generates sympathy and media interest, how do lobbyists and the interests they represent make politicians feel the heat so that they may see the light, as Everett Dirksen so aptly put it?

Just producing volumes of phone calls and letters doesn't do the trick. Everyone knows they can be generated by the ton, if one has enough money, and don't necessarily represent the kind of heated interest that will sway politicians. The key is to generate interest and activity among what are called "significant constituents"—persons that politicians consider to be key elements of their political base by dint of their personal authority and/or ability to generate or contribute substantial amounts of campaign money and whose presence is central to the politician's career.

That there are such things as "significant constituents" stems from the undemocratic notion that everyone is not considered equal in politics. Just as certain states may merit more campaign time and money than others during presidential contests, because their electoral votes cannot be taken for granted by either party, politicians look at constituents—whether voters or campaign contributors or both—as members of particular blocs. They and their consultants create dozens of categories, defined by party, ideology, voting propensity, income level, gender, ethnicity, age, or membership in some economic group, such as labor union members, farmers, or business persons. In a state as diverse as California, these pigeonholes are potentially infinite in number and one person may easily fit into two or more of them. Within each bloc is a small core of leaders who can represent its interests accurately and sway others within the bloc. The key to any political career is understanding the motivations of these constituent groups and their leaders and becoming at least minimally responsive to them.

To serve his clients the lobbyist identifies those within a politician's bailiwick who are friendly to the cause and influential with the politician. The lobbyist helps his client and the targeted politician by fostering a relationship between the two, gaining a conduit for his message and lubricating the relationship between a politician and the representative of an influential group. That's the essence of grassroots organization, although it takes other forms as well, both public and private.

A garden-variety significant constituent is a registered voter, preferably of the legislator's party, who votes consistently for the politician, who will promote the politician among friends and associates, and volunteers useful information to the officeholder or candidate about conditions or issues.

A very significant constituent embodies all the qualities of the first level, but may become a public endorser or campaigner for the politician, makes at least small campaign contributions, perhaps volunteers in a campaign, and acts as a public defender of and advocate for the politician as needed.

The third level of significance is reached when the constituent takes a more active role in campaigns by hosting a fundraising event, arranges for the politician to make speeches to his or her organizations, regularly attends fundraising events, visits the Capitol occasionally, and perhaps serves on a legislator's campaign finance or steering committee.

At the fourth and highest level of significance, the constituent becomes an active part of the politician's support network, engineers support, and perhaps financial contributions, from an important district interest group, makes or arranges campaign contributions in the multi-thousand-dollar range, facilitates meetings with major financial or political players, and/or becomes an officer in the legislator's party.

A legislator will knock himself out to maintain friendly relations with anyone in the second and third levels of significance and will sell his mother's soul to take care of those in the fourth level, the "true blues," as it were. Lobbyists want to either help those friendly to his clients' interests achieve significant constituent status or identify those already in such exalted positions and enlist them in the cause. If certain lobbyists achieve reputations for rarely losing any fight—reputations that bring them more clients and retainer fees—it's because they have developed this third leg of the stool so completely.

We aren't talking about a great many people in a state of 35 million people. A typical state Senate district has perhaps 850,000 residents, of whom 60 percent are eligible voters (over the age of 18 and citizens) and 45 percent are registered voters (although this number can vary widely, depending on the ethnicity and economic status of the community). Of 400,000 or so registered voters, 300,000 will vote in a typical election.

A state senator is personally acquainted, perhaps, with a couple of thousand of his voters. And of those, a few hundred may be considered truly significant and perhaps a few dozen can be considered true-blue, fourth-level constituents who always get their phone calls returned and who can generally count on the senator's vote if crunch time comes. Identifying and adroitly employing at least some of those few dozen is the lobbyist's goal as he analyzes his client's interests, the role that a legislator plays in furthering or retarding those interests and the influence that significant constituents may play.

Sometimes it's relatively easy. If one is lobbying for agricultural interests and the targeted lawmaker represents a rural, farm district—and might even be a farmer himself—getting access and a sympathetic hearing is a slam dunk. But if one is helping farmers and the key legislative vote is held by a Latino legislator with liberal leanings and connections to environmentalists or the United Farm Workers Union, it's much tougher to identify significant constituents whose phone calls or visits can make a difference. One example of networking oozed into the public prints in 1999—a rarity unto itself—when a memorandum from a lobbyist for the Grocery Manufacturers of America was leaked. The lobbyists, one of many fighting a war over deposits on beverage containers, talked about hiring "Davis influentials" who had the ear of Governor Gray Davis and who could persuade him to veto the environmentalist-backed "bottle bill" if it reached his desk. Several long-time acquaintances of and/or former aides to the governor were placed on the opposition payroll.

Effective grassroots organization can play a vital role in the first step of persuading a lawmaker to take a position favorable to a lobbyists' client: gaining access. All the arguments in the world, whether based on merit or raw political advantage, won't work if the lobbyist cannot gain the legislator's ear. But if the politician knows, or at least suspects, that the lobbyist has organized significant constituents in his or her district and can speak for them, access becomes easier. Once access is gained—wherever that may be—the lobbyist can reinforce his standing by persuading the politician that cooperation will generate personal and/or financial support at election time. And, of course, access means that the lobbyist has an opportunity to make his argument on its merits and provide the legislator with information, either about the issue itself or about its political aspects.

If a legislator knows that significant constituents in her district are monitoring her votes, speeches, and other activities on a particular issue, the chances are those actions favor the constituents' position. That doesn't happen unless the lobbyist keeps those key persons informed, motivates them to contact their lawmakers, and then follows through by producing political support from those constituents when campaign time comes. If a legislator listens and responds to influential constituents, he's more likely to cooperate with the lobbyist who organizes constituent action.

Once a lobbyist's ability to generate grassroots support is established, he needn't activate the network on every issue. As with the ability to generate and deliver campaign contributions, one's reputation is often powerful enough to carry the day.

Developing, maintaining, and servicing a grassroots organization is expensive, time-consuming, and often frustrating work, because it basically is a process of training or education. For large organizations with multiple issues pending in the Legislature, it's often a full-time staff job—or jobs. It's trickier business for the contract lobbyist, who's hired to deal with only one aspect of a client's political involvement and may be dependent on an organizational effort over which he exercises little or no control. But grassroots organization has become so important with the arrival of term-limited legislators who retain strong ties to their districts that Sacramento has seen a virtual explosion of pubic relations firms offering to generate grassroots support or opposition on legislative issues. That said, how does one go about creating a grassroots organization that can deliver the support that a lobbyist needs to win? Here are the general principles and basic components:

- Political issues don't exist in a vacuum. At any one moment, there are dozens of other issues, some related and some not, also pending, and they may interact with one another in unpredictable ways. Constituency organization efforts must adapt to the precise circumstances of the issue at hand.
- Operatives who may be whizzes at organizing political campaigns are not necessarily adept at directing a grassroots campaign on a legislative issue. Effective grassroots organization is a skill that must be acquired clinically—on the job—not didactically.
- It's expensive business. Creating a good grassroots effort on one legislative issue can easily cost over a half-million dollars for personal time, travel, and ancillary expenses.
- Good internal communications, usually through written materials, is vital. At the onset of any grassroots drive someone who knows how to write clearly and with a minimum of jargon must prepare basic materials that include the definition of the issue and the organization's position, supporting arguments, opposition arguments and responses, objective studies and other data that bolster the organization's position. A full-fledged international communications campaign might include videos, an Internet website, and a network of email addresses.
- Another basic is a socio-economic and political profile of the legislative district of every lawmaker targeted for influence. The data, often but not always available off-the-shelf, from public and private sources, include major components of the local economic base, local civic and political organizations that might play vital roles, the names and contact information of opinion and political leaders, voter registration and voting profiles, and local organizations that might have a direct stake in the outcome of the issue.

- Opinion research, conducted through polling and focus groups, is another basic for effective grassroots action in any truly high-stakes political battle. To gain an understanding of the client's strengths, the potency or vulnerabilities of the opposition, and the effectiveness of themes, one must know how voters, especially those in the districts of legislators targeted for opinion-molding, view the issue, both in terms of general awareness and preconceived positions. Polling also provides an opportunity to test the political standing of the politicians involved, which can play a role in approaches.

- A scorecard categorizes legislators involved in the issue as to their preexisting positions, if any, their levels of friendliness or hostility to the interest groups involved, and their potential susceptibility to grassroots influence. The notion is to produce a list of targeted legislators and to generate the requisite number of votes to pass or defeat the legislation at issue.

- Once the basic research is done and the field of battle is well-defined, targeted legislators and their districts should be divvied up among grassroots coordinators, each of whom handle 10–25 districts in a statewide effort. They, in turn, recruit regional coordinators, either professionals or talented amateurs with experience in political campaigns or similar activities and some expertise in local economic, social, and political dynamics—who know the lay of the land. The network of coordinators needs a good two-way system of gathering and disseminating information, a task made much easier in the electronic age. Coordinators must have a realistic set of goals, on whose progress they report regularly.

- Forming a coalition of supporting involves one-on-one meetings with groups that could, or should, be brought into the battle because their interests are similar or intertwined. The supporting organizations and the significant constituents become part of a key contact database that can be activated instantaneously to contact lawmakers, make public pronouncements, or fill in holes that inevitably arise in any campaign.

- The public face of the grassroots campaign includes recruitment and training of speakers for service clubs and other forums, using written materials, videos and talking points to paint a picture of imminent crisis and the need for action. Grassroots coordinators find venues for the speakers—which is usually not difficult, given the hundreds of luncheon organizations and their insatiable appetites for speakers.

- Another public face is what's generally called "A Day in Sacramento." Volunteer members of a trade association or other interest group descend on the Capitol to listen to pep talks from their leaders, background information from their lobbyists, and speeches from friendly politicians, perhaps a dinner or a reception, and massive visits to individual legislators' offices, either to talk to the officials themselves or aides as high up on the organizational chart as they can find. Setting up such an event, which may involve hundreds or even thousands of people, can be a logistical task of daunting proportions, involving transportation, hotel reservations, meeting spaces, appointments with lawmakers, information packets, and speakers' schedules. And it can create more resentment than positive response if not handled adroitly, with the amateur lobbyists focused on the specific cause at hand. But if they become annual events, those involved usually become more adept at their staging and they can be valuable adjuncts to professional lobbying, especially in dealing with inexperienced, term-limited lawmakers.

- The media campaign must involve professional consultants experienced in the ways of the press, which are often mysterious to outsiders. A serious, statewide effort must have an experienced media spokesman—a "flack" in the parlance of the journalistic trade, often a former reporter—who can operate both proactively and reactively. Proactively, the media consultant or, more likely consultants, may prepare and distribute press packets, arrange for news conferences for major announcements, deal with selected journalists one-on-one to establish relationships that may be useful for leaking material injurious to the opposition, contact editorial boards of newspapers to solicit editorial support, write news releases and op-ed pieces that are offered to newspapers under the name of the public leader of the campaign, schedule campaign principals for radio and television talk shows, prepare audio and video feeds for broadcast outlets, and oversee, if necessary, a paid advertising campaign.

- Public and private pats on the back for friendly politicians are another tool in the grassroots campaign designer's box of tricks. When a legislator commits to the desired side of the issue, it reinforces that commitment—and guards against any reneging—by having it acknowledged through press announcements, billboards emblazoned with effusive thanks, and perhaps private meetings or dinners with significant constituents who have been enlisted in the effort. Politicians, more than most people, seems to need such positive feedback. It's also important to protect the committed lawmaker against reprisals by the opposition through pledges of personal and financial campaign support. A district-based fundraiser is an important component of the reinforcement mechanism, especially if the politician believes that he or she has been damaged by making a commitment. A variation on the theme arose in 2000 when the California Water Association, a lobbying organization for privately owned water companies, supplied 25,000 Thanksgiving turkeys to members of the Legislature, who could then donate them to local charities or needy families and reap the favorable publicity for their cost-free acts of altruism. Political reformer Jim Knox described the practice as "a pretty creative way for lobbyists or agencies who lobby the Capitol to curry favor with legislators."

Not only are term-limited legislators more susceptible to grassroots political pressure than their professional predecessors, but the way in which campaign money flows has also changed with the evolution of Capitol culture, becoming less centralized in the hands of legislative leaders, more diffused and local. Smart, adaptive interest groups don't simply write big checks to legislative leaders and allow them to distribute the money as they please. Not only are the leaders weaker under term limits, not always able to deliver on their promises to lobbyists, but the frequent turnover of legislators is inherently destabilizing. Interest group lobbyists and organizers have to spend more time gathering local intelligence, figuring out which potential legislative candidates are in the pipeline, and cultivating them with personal contacts and timely campaign contributions, sometimes in city council or school board races, to gain pre-legislative influence. Grassroots organizing and campaign money distribution have become more intertwined, both occurring less in Sacramento and more in hometowns of legislators or potential candidates.

As it has evolved, it's a new age version of Artie Samish's old "select and elect" system and a dramatic turnabout of the three decades in which legislative bosses such as Unruh and Brown centralized the collection and disbursement of campaign funds and called the shots. The passage of Proposition 34 in 2000 takes legislative leaders out of the campaign financing picture even more. Drafted by the Legislature itself to effectively overturn a more draconian campaign finance reform measure passed by voters, but stalled in the courts, Proposition 34 imposes limits on direct contributions to legislators and legislative candidates and transfers from legislative leaders, but allows money to flow with few restrictions through state parties. While state party leaders would become more powerful figures under the measure, it indirectly, and perhaps inadvertently, invited interest groups to organize fundraising and campaign money distribution at the local level and "bundle" their contributions to make their interest group origins clear. It made old-style, one-on-one, leadership-oriented lobbying even less relevant.

A starkly dramatic example of how lobbying in Sacramento evolved during the 1990s was the conflict between medical care providers and personal injury attorneys over the 1975-vintage, $250,000 ceiling on pain and suffering damages in medical malpractice cases, itself the product of an early and effective grassroots lobbying campaign. (A full disclosure note: both authors of this book have connections to the issue. Jay Michael for many years was the chief lobbyist for the California Medical Association, which gained passage of the malpractice cap in 1975, and later became head of Californians Allied for Patient Protection (CAPP), the specific organization set up by medical providers to defend the cap against efforts of personal injury attorneys to repeal or raise it. Dan Walters covered the issue as a journalist beginning in 1975 and his daughter, Danielle Walters, took over as CAPP's chief staffer after Michael retired.)

The now-famous—or infamous—"napkin deal" on personal injury lawsuits, hammered out in 1987 during hours of negotiations in the Capitol and later at Frank Fat's, included a five-year moratorium in the political war between medical care providers and personal injury lawyers on the 1975-vintage, $250,000 ceiling on pain and suffering damages in medical malpractice cases. When the truce expired in the early 1990s, there was not an immediate resumption of hostilities. The speaker of the state Assembly at the time, the legendary Willie Brown, was a key architect of the napkin deal and was not particularly interested in carrying water for the trial attorneys, and Republican Governor Pete Wilson would almost certainly veto any legislation that repealed or substantially raised the $250,000 cap. The lawyers still wanted action on a provision that had cost them hundreds of millions of dollars in contingency fees, but they had to wait a few years to make their move.

During the moratorium and the lull that followed, medical care providers, led by the California Medical Association, created a specialized lobby, Californians Allied for Patient Protection (CAPP), to defend the malpractice cap. And a major CAPP goal was to create a grassroots support network that would help when the truce ended, as everyone knew it would.

The CAPP grassroots effort took several forms, but three of the most important were to identify members of the Legislature, particularly Democrats, who had ties to the medical care industry, to provide money and other support for legislative candidates CAPP believed would be sympathetic to their position, and to enlist organizations and interest groups that would be effective with the Legislature's dominant Democrats. All three drives intertwined with one another—occurred in a period when the Legislature itself was undergoing cultural change. Terms limits had created an era of rapid turnover, when about a third of the Legislature would change every election cycle, and that meant frequent changes of legislative leaders, committee chairs and key staffers as well. Term limits meant that lawmakers were less likely to be experienced Capitol staffers—the chief occupation of legislators during the pre-term limits era—and more likely to be graduates of local governments and civic life. The rapid turnover also meant that the numbers of women and ethnic minorities, especially Latinos, would increase sharply. As it turned out, the late 1990s also saw Democrats increase their hold on the Capitol, which should have been a boost for the personal injury lawyers, whose political connections were to Democratic leaders.

Medical lobbyists were pleasantly surprised to learn, as they delved into backgrounds of the Capitol newcomers, that there were a large number of members with health care connections. Many of the new women were former nurses, some legislators were married to doctors or other medical providers, and many of those who had spent time in local government had overseen medical care programs and been sued themselves in malpractice cases. Assuming that they could count on Republicans in a showdown with the trial lawyers, the medical lobbyists focused on Democrats, hoping to undercut the money-oriented appeal that lawyers would make to post-Brown legislative leaders. That focus carried into the drive to cultivate candidates in Democratic primaries that had become less controlled by party leaders in Sacramento and more oriented toward local financial and political support.

The most public face of the CAPP grassroots campaign was the coalition of allied interest groups that could influence Democrats, such as women's reproductive health clinics and inner-city health facilities. They pounded home the message that raising the costs of malpractice insurance, the inevitable effect of abolishing or expanding the pain and suffering cap, would mean fewer health services for women, minorities, and the poor. CAPP organizers traveled the state constantly, keeping in touch with local medical groups and urging them to remain in contact with legislators, while gathering intelligence on local political landscapes and cultivating potential candidates for the Legislature.

The personal injury attorneys, who were undergoing some internal discord over malpractice strategy and other issues, did not adapt as rapidly or as completely to the Capitol's much-changed atmosphere. They continued to rely primarily on their Sacramento connections, especially to the Democratic speakers who served in two-year stints after Willie Brown's departure, and on money funneled through those leaders. But the weakness of that strategy became evident when two speakers, Cruz Bustamante and Antonio Villaraigosa, failed to persuade their own caucuses to support the lawyers on lifting the malpractice cap. While CAPP lobbyists trotted out their Democrat-friendly allies at public hearings on the issue, the grassroots cultivation of Democrats was the key factor in blocking the trial lawyers inside the Democratic caucus.

No small part of that cultivation was the judicious and localized application of campaign money, collected from doctors, hospitals and other medical care providers, which is an integral part of a successful grassroots drive—especially in an era of term limits and restrictions on direct injections of campaign funds from Sacramento-based "political action committees" or PACs, which proliferated during the 1970s and 1980s as part of the centralization of legislative politics.

As term limits took hold in the 1970s, CAPP began decentralizing its own campaign contribution program. While retaining its centralized PAC operations in Sacramento, it supplemented it with a series of locally staged fundraising events aimed at assisting legislators known to be friendly to CAPP's position on malpractice limits or cultivating lawmakers and candidates considered to be potential allies. CAPP would sponsor local fundraisers, pick up the out-of-pocket costs for organizational work and catering, and encourage local members of its coalition to purchase modestly priced tickets. It invited executives of allied groups—such as publicly owned health facilities or charitable organizations—that were barred by law from making campaign contributions, allowing them to bootstrap on the contributors to obtain access to legislators. These frequent events put campaign money into the treasuries of friendly legislators, solidified the connection between that money and the "significant constituents" who would attend the event, and enhanced the standing of CAPP's Sacramento lobbyists, who would usually make appearances. Thus, the events encapsulated all three legs of the potent political action campaign.

CAPP's rivals, the Consumer Attorneys of California who wanted to lift the malpractice cap, weren't idle during the 1990s, as they geared up for a renewal of the perennial war. But they were beset by internal discord over goals and tactics, not only on the malpractice issue but other political matters, and continued to largely funnel money to legislative leaders, or to allow individual law firms to make contributions directly, without the coordination that CAPP maintained. The effectiveness of the CAPP approach when confronting a trial lawyer lobby once considered invincible was indirectly acknowledged after voters in 2000 enacted, Proposition 34. By imposing limits on direct contributions from PACs, Proposition 34 indirectly encouraged the bifurcated system that CAPP had perfected. Other interest groups scrambled to set up their own systems combining grassroots organization with locally based fundraising that would not count against PAC contribution limits—a sophisticated form of "bundling" that had arisen in federal elections after restrictions on donations were imposed in the mid-1970s.

CHAPTER 7

A Year of Living Dangerously

*"We're the good guys here"—recycling lobbyist Mark Murray, when
confronted with charges that his beverage deposit bill would take food
out of the mouths of babies.*

On the Road in California, 1987[1]

Everything Mark Murray needed to know about politics he could have learned
from the lowly wine cooler. He just didn't realize it at the time. If he had, he
might not have spent the next 12 years fighting battle after battle against some of

[1]This chapter was written by Dan Weintraub, adapted from a series of articles he
wrote for *The Orange County Register* in 2000. It is included in this book to demonstrate,
in fine detail, the severe limitations on what public interest lobbyists can accomplish in
the contemporary California Capitol, largely because they cannot by law or circumstances participate in the single most important aspect of lobbying: making campaign
contributions. Nor can they readily finance the extensive media and grassroots work that
usually accompanies a successful lobbying campaign. By underscoring the limits on public interest lobbyists, this chapter illustrates the themes that money drives public policy,
that special interest lobbyists control political decision making in their fields, and that
their victories often come at the expense of what many would consider the larger public
interest.

the most influential special interests in California, and against his conscience. But in the summer of 1987 Murray was just a few months out of college, a skinny kid with shaggy brown hair who found himself in the middle of one of the biggest environmental issues of his time.

Murray was crisscrossing the state for a fledgling nonprofit group, laying ambush to the bigger but less nimble California wine industry. Driving a blue Chevy wagon he'd borrowed from his parents, wearing the dark suit his father bought him as a graduation gift, Murray was trying to persuade city councils to place a nickel deposit on every wine cooler sold in their towns.

The bottle deposits were designed to boost recycling in the cities that adopted them. They were also weapons in a larger war under way in the halls of the state Capitol.

It was a war Murray felt lucky to be in. At Humboldt State University, on California's rugged north coast, he'd been surrounded by radicals trying to save the earth. He enjoyed the majestic redwoods as much as anyone, but he didn't know an Italian cypress from a madrone. His passion was politics. His class-mates elected him student-body president. Even before he graduated, he helped run a local pol's campaign for county supervisor.

He arrived in Sacramento an unsure 24-year-old, not knowing what kind of job he might land. He didn't seek out recycling, much less know that it would become an obsession. He sort of stumbled into it, hearing through a friend that Californians Against Waste was looking for an intern.

It was a smart move. Recycling looked like The Next Big Thing. A garbage barge, floating off the Atlantic coast for months in search of a place to dump its cargo, drew international attention to the cause. Landfills were filling up and shutting down. Kids and old folks and a lot of people in between were talking about what they could do to reduce, reuse, recycle.

Recycling was the perfect issue for Murray because it provided battles he saw as winnable—not like saving the whales or shutting down nuclear power. And Murray loved to compete. As a fifth-grader back in Buffalo, he once scored three goals in a hockey game, then shed his pads for a figure skater's outfit and performed the Dutch waltz in a pairs competition with a neighbor girl. In high school, he turned to distance running and became a marathon champion. Six years later he was still a dedicated runner. He ran hard, and he ran to win. That's how he did everything.

When the Legislature passed the state's first bottle recycling bill in 1986, requiring deposits and refunds on soda, beer, and carbonated water, the wine industry used its clout to gain an exemption for its bottles. The wineries, like most other beverage makers, opposed anything that added a cost to consumers at the checkout line.

But what about wine coolers, a fizzy mix of wine, juice, and fruit flavoring that had become popular almost overnight? Gallo made its Bartles & Jaymes brand famous with a sappy ad campaign featuring Frank and Ed. Seagram had its own brand, pitched by Bruce Willis. Californians, especially women, were buying the new drinks by the millions. Recycling advocates argued that coolers were closer to soda pop than to wine, and legislation was proposed to add the bottles to the recycling program. The bill, however, stalled in the Legislature.

Murray's boss, Bill Shireman, sat him down in the shabby offices that Californians Against Waste rented near the Capitol. Like a father explaining the facts of life to his son, Shireman told Murray how Sacramento really worked.

The Legislature, he said, will never cross the wine industry. The lawmakers were simply too dependent on the money the wineries contributed to their campaigns. The only way to win is to get the wineries to back down. Then the legislators will go along. We can do that, Shireman said, by persuading cities from San Diego to Arcata to pass a patchwork of bottle-deposit laws. Big industries prefer their politics simple and concentrated. Spread them out, skirmish with them on many small fronts, and the wineries will see a single, statewide standard as the better way to go.

So Murray hit the road, sitting late into the night in small, cramped council chambers in strange towns, waiting his turn as the locals debated traffic lights and condominium projects. He won in Davis and Santa Monica, in Imperial Beach and Los Angeles. Even in Moreno Valley, in the fast-growing and conservative suburbs east of Riverside, Murray prevailed. When the city council voted his way, he found a phone and called his boss. If we can win in Moreno Valley, Murray told Shireman, we can win anywhere. This was no Santa Monica. This is like the American heartland. And they sided with us!

Murray was right. Before the year was out, a half-dozen cities had adopted the deposit laws he was pushing. Another dozen were considering it. Early in 1988, the industry caved. Soon after, the Legislature passed a bill requiring bottle deposits on wine coolers.

It looked like a great grass-roots victory: The little guys beat Big Wine. But Murray knew it wasn't really David against Goliath. The whole thing was paid for by donations from Coors and Anheuser-Busch—the wineries' competition. The model ordinances Murray shopped to the cities were written by beer industry lawyers. The big breweries helped out because beer bottles already carried a deposit. They did not want the wine coolers getting a free ride.

But the wine cooler would be the last beverage added to the recycling program. Murray would try and fail for more than a decade to convince the Legislature to expand the program further. As those years passed, he often drew on the lessons he learned from the wine cooler episode: Your enemies one day might be your allies the next. Ideals are no more than pleasant thoughts unless you win. To win in Sacramento, you need powerful friends.

Above all, he learned that the fight over recycling, by the time it reached the Capitol, wasn't really about the environment anymore. It was all about money.

Sacramento, August 1998

Murray folded his hands in front of him and stared at them. He tried not to look up as Senator John Burton's face grew redder. One thing Murray had learned in his years as a lobbyist was that when John Burton got angry, you stayed out of his way. Ask him for anything during one of his tantrums and you were more likely to lose something instead.

Murray figured he had lost enough in the 11 years since he came to the Capitol straight out of school. He was no longer the scruffy college grad barnstorming the state in his parents' station wagon. Now he was a registered lobbyist, urging lawmakers to expand California's recycling program by requiring deposits on more bottles and cans. Year after year he'd failed, defeated by interest groups with more money, better connections, and more clout. But he never gave up. He remained a distance runner, disciplined and whippet-thin, accustomed to the long haul. And his drive to expand recycling, once just a job, had become an obsession. It was his political marathon.

With the legislative session coming to a close, Murray suspected that 1998 was not going to be the year for radical reform. But he hoped to make some progress. He managed to insert a small but important provision into a bill Burton was putting together. It would double deposits to five cents on the 20-ounce plastic bottles that Coke and Pepsi were selling like crazy. With that kind of incentive—they called it the "nickel-20"—far more of those bottles would be recycled rather than ending up in landfills and on freeway shoulders.

Murray was one of about a dozen lobbyists Burton summoned to a large wooden table in his conference room, an ornately decorated chamber befitting the leader of the state Senate and the most powerful member of the Legislature. The glass industry was there, and beer and wine and trash and soft drinks. The supermarkets' lobbyist was in the room, and the recycling centers had a couple of seats at the table. They were gathered because California's recycling program, once the handsome child of the state's environmental movement, had become an awkward adolescent. It was now in many ways an unwieldy jumble of special-interest deals. The program took $400 million in bottle deposits and fees from consumers and beverage makers and paid it out to trash haulers, recycling centers, environmental groups, and people who returned their beverage containers for a refund. The whole thing generated enough fees, subsidies, and rules to keep 25 or 30 lobbyists employed.

Now, in the summer of 1998, most of the program was about to expire. Burton's bill was written to keep the money flowing to the special interests for another year. The lobbyists, seeing an opportunity, tried to tack on provisions that would help their clients. They bickered as they jostled for position, testing Burton's patience. Murray believed in open government. But he also needed to fight for his interests. So he was glad to be in that room.

He thought he had Burton on his side. But he knew the senator's help would not come without risk. Burton was neither a master of detail nor an environmental idealist. When he talked about recycling, it was to recall how he and his childhood pals would steal bottles from the back of the neighborhood market and take them around to the front of the store for a refund.

Above all, Burton was a deal-cutter—and a great one. He was interested in this issue mainly because some of the most influential interest groups in the Capitol had a stake in it. Murray could not know what would happen if the concerns of one of those interest groups clashed with what he thought was best for the environment.

Burton had heard enough squabbling. He began to rant. Murray studied the ridges in his palms. Burton snarled, "If someone has a complaint, let me know now and I won't waste my time." Bruce Young, the retailers' lobbyist, whispered something to the man sitting next to him. Burton caught it. "Come on, Brucie," Burton teased Young, taunting the beefy lobbyist by using the diminutive form of his name—a Burton trademark. "Tell me what it is. I'm gonna find out anyway. Tell me now."

Young ducked Burton's jab. "Lee Johnson has a concern," he said. Johnson was the president of 20/20 Recycling, one of the companies that operated recycling centers in supermarket parking lots across the state. Burton's glare swung to Johnson. The problem, Johnson said, was that his company needed a long-term deal—three years at least. He was going to the banks to finance an expansion. They'd balk if the state subsidies his company was getting through the existing bottle bill were not assured for longer than one year. If you can't do that, Johnson said, his group couldn't support this bill.

That was it. "I'll save you the trouble," Burton seethed. Then he slid back his chair and, putting his hands on the table, pushed himself up to his full 6 foot 1. "FUCK YOU ALL!!!" the senator roared. And he strode from the room. The lobbyists were dumbfounded. Was he serious? They couldn't be sure. Two ran down the hall after Burton, calmed him down and coaxed him back into the room. This guy is nuts, Murray said to himself. He's got all these lobbyists in here—professionals, attorneys, even former legislators—and he's got them scared. But he got them to quit their bickering. They were in awe of him. Murray was too.

Burton dismissed the lobbyists and returned to the Senate floor. The bill would not be changed. It passed in Burton's Senate, and in the Assembly. But Governor Pete Wilson vetoed the bill. His complaint: He didn't like the proposal to increase deposits on 20-ounce bottles. Murray's precious "nickel-20" had sunk the entire deal. But he wasn't worried. Wilson's veto threatened to throw the recycling program into chaos. More than $50 million in government subsidies were going to expire. The companies that depended on those payments were now desperate. In their desperation, Murray sensed opportunity.

Sacramento, December 1998

This was the moment Murray had been waiting for since coming to the Capitol to work for Californians Against Waste. He had climbed from intern to policy director and then to executive director in his 11 years at the nonprofit group. All that time he'd been pushing bills to expand recycling. Every year he'd failed. But now a new governor—Democrat Gray Davis—was about to take office. A new Legislature with more members sympathetic to the environment had just been seated. And Kip Lipper, an aide to Senator Byron Sher, was on the phone.

Lipper told Murray that Sher wanted to carry the bill in the Legislature. The Senate leader, Burton, would lend his clout. And Lipper wanted Murray to help draft the measure. "Start with 468," Lipper said, referring to the recycling bill Governor Wilson vetoed a few months before leaving office. "Add in expansion."

Murray knew what Lipper meant—their long-held desire to require deposits and refunds on two billion cans and bottles a year not covered by the state's recycling program. The bill also would include Murray's proposal to double the deposit—to a nickel—on the increasingly popular 20-ounce plastic bottles of soda.

This was the dream assignment. It wasn't totally unexpected, given his expertise on the issue, but Murray was nonetheless flattered. As Sacramento lobbyists went, he was small-time. His nonprofit group had a few thousand members. He rode to work on a mountain bike, not in a Lexus. He carried a canvas backpack instead of a Coach valise. And while his friends included some of the Capitol's most successful lobbyists, men and women with long lists of corporate clients and incomes that reached toward seven figures, Murray had chosen not to play that game. But he was a man of no small ego. He wanted to be somebody, to be a part of the action. He was tired of being on the outside. This would be a rare chance for him to leave at least some small mark on history.

Becoming an insider, however, carried certain obligations. He and Burton and Sher all shared the same goal. But to reach it, the senators might be tempted to cut deals with special interests that Murray loathed. If they did, he realized, he would have to go along. That was the way the Capitol worked.

The first unpleasant deal, an unspoken one, presented itself almost immediately. Murray worked on the bill for several days, sitting at his computer in a cluttered sixth-floor office overlooking Cesar Chavez Park, and Sacramento City Hall. On the floor around his desk he spread manila folders containing previous drafts of bills, newspaper clippings, and policy papers he had been saving for years. He cranked up his favorite rock radio station and worked late into the night, finding a use for old deals that had long been searching for a home. He would eventually give his draft to Lipper, who would present it to Senator Sher. That was commonplace around the Capitol, where the lobbyists served as a sort of unpaid staff to the legislators. The members, of course, had the final say, as

Sher would with this bill. But it was not unheard of for a lobbyist-written provision to find its way into a bill without anyone in the Legislature realizing it was there.

This bill would rope in Snapple, Gatorade, Frappuccino—and all the iced teas, coffees, and fruit drinks invented since the original law was enacted in 1986. No longer would spring water be exempted while consumers paid deposits on carbonated water. Fruit-flavored drinks without bubbles would now carry the same deposit as fruit-flavored sodas sold in identical containers. It seemed a rather modest proposal to Murray, not something that should take more than 10 years to accomplish. Not something that should take over a person's life. But then, there was nothing easy about going up against the California wine industry.

Murray had long advocated deposits on wine so that more people would recycle the containers. His group sponsored bill after bill targeting the beverage. One year they went after all wine bottles. That failed. Next they tried for just the "fortified" wines—Thunderbird, Ripple—favored by street people. That failed, too. They even drafted a ballot initiative. But they couldn't get any financial backing. The wine industry, which fought anything that would increase the price of its product to consumers, was too strong.

Given that history, Murray now felt it was hopeless to even suggest that the senators include wine bottles in this bill. Lawmakers collected millions in campaign contributions from the wineries and did not want to cross them. Even Senator Burton, the Legislature's most powerful member, would not challenge wine.

Burton's position was driven home for Murray one day shortly after Lipper's call. That morning, Murray was quoted in a newspaper article—misquoted, he thought—suggesting the bill he was drafting might require deposits on wine bottles. He arrived in his office to find a scathing message on his answering machine. It was from one of Burton's aides. "What are you doing?" she asked. Murray cringed. Her tone said: Are you crazy? Murray was not crazy. He knew wine had to remain exempt if the bill were to survive. But he was troubled that it wasn't even going to be the subject of public debate. We're wusses, he thought. But he'd given ground already, without even putting up a fight. Sometimes the most significant thing about a bill is not what you put in it but what you leave out. On days like this he would stop by after work to see Heather Strauch, a Sacramento lawyer. An acquaintance for years, she would become his girlfriend, and his sounding board, as he pushed his bill through the Legislature. Murray loved to cook, and he would often fix her dinner after unwinding with a long evening run through the tree-lined streets of her old Sacramento neighborhood.

"Can I tell you about my day?" he would say, his face twisted in frustration, as he stood at her kitchen sink staring out the window into the darkness. They both knew he would tell her about his day whether she wanted to hear it or not. Murray felt helpless to change the Capitol's priorities. The best he could hope for was to work the system to his advantage by trying to get the big contributors to support his bill. And who better to turn to first for support, Murray was thinking, than your oldest and most bitter opponent?

The Capitol, January 1999

Murray had always heard that politics made strange bedfellows. He was about to find out what it was like to be under the covers. For his entire career Murray had been fighting the two companies that manufactured almost every glass bottle sold in California. He was the state's most committed advocate for recycling. They wanted nothing less than to repeal huge chunks of the state's recycling program. Now, Murray found himself doing the unthinkable—asking the glass companies to help him expand recycling. But as it turned out, they now needed Murray as much as he needed them. They stood to lose millions of dollars if his bill did not pass by the end of the year. So as the 1999 legislative session dawned, Murray was seated across the table from Alan L. Edelstein, the chief lobbyist for the glass-bottle industry.

The two men closeted themselves in a tiny second-floor conference room overlooking the Capitol's east steps, where towering English elms marked the old oval carriage track to the Statehouse doors. They were there on the orders of Senator Burton. The Senate leader, through his aides, had let Murray know he was willing to help him expand recycling by requiring deposits on billions of bottles and cans long exempt from California's law. But Burton wanted this done without harming the glass industry. He didn't really care how they did it. He just wanted Murray and Edelstein to come together. They could write almost anything they pleased as long as the two of them agreed on it.

Edelstein, an owlish man whose stiff brown hair was always trimmed neatly above his ears, was about 15 years Murray's senior and had twice as much experience in the Capitol. A lawyer by training and an undergrad at Berkeley in its antiwar heyday, he could argue persuasively for whatever point he was trying to make. But like many good lawyers Murray knew, he didn't seem to have a personal interest in the causes he pushed. Clients told him what they needed. His job was to get it done.

Murray could never do that. He knew he could earn a lot more than $60,000 a year if he did. Edelstein was pulling in six figures from glass alone—and they were just one client. But Murray needed to work for a cause he believed in. And he didn't want to take orders from anyone. He considered Edelstein an honorable guy. He just worked for dinosaurs—the glassmakers. Their employees came off like a bunch of union goons who loved to scream and shout, even when they didn't know what they were talking about. Once, one of them pinned the 150-pound Murray against a wall in a Capitol hallway, poked a finger into his chest and hollered at him, blaming him for the loss of hundreds of jobs.

The target of the glass industry's anger was a concept that lay at the heart of the state's recycling program but was invisible to the general public. Designed by the man who gave Murray his start in the Capitol, Bill Shireman, it was a simple idea that put California on the cutting edge of the environmental movement: require beverage companies to foot the bill for the pollution their products cause. Bottles were charged what amounted to a pollution tax. The state used the money to subsidize hundreds of little companies that collected, sorted, cleaned and shipped the bottles back to the factories to be melted down and used again. The fees drove up the cost of drinks sold in bottles. The idea was to nudge consumers toward beverages sold in environmentally friendlier aluminum cans.

Murray had spent 12 years defending and refining his old mentor's legacy, and he thought the system made perfect sense. It worked so well, in fact, that the glass companies blamed it for the industry's decline. In 1995, the Legislature took pity and cut the fees—temporarily. Without that break, the industry would be paying nearly $50 million a year; instead, the fees were closer to $12 million. But that deal was about to expire. Edelstein was paid to keep it alive.

Edelstein's opening offer was bold: The glass companies would support Murray's bill, but they needed to hang on to the break they had. And they wanted a bigger one. Murray knew Edelstein had the clout to keep the status quo. Edelstein's other clients included the city of San Francisco—Senator Burton's hometown—and the two men had grown close while working together to defend the city's interests. Now those ties were coming in handy for Edelstein.

This grated on Murray. He'd given his blessing, reluctantly, when the glass companies won their break a few years before. At the time, he feared the industry would succeed in unraveling the whole program if its complaints were not addressed. But he saw no need to give glass an even better deal, at least not without getting something in return. So he countered Edelstein: The fees would drop, Murray suggested, but only if more glass bottles were recycled. That was a bargain he could square with his ideals. It would be a marriage of environmental goals and market incentives. Edelstein was intrigued. But he gave Murray his usual answer: He'd have to get back to him.

Over the next few days Murray tried to win over the Senate aides who he was working with on the bill. He exchanged a couple of phone calls with Edelstein. But he was getting nowhere. It was clear the glass guys did not like the idea.

A few weeks later, Edelstein was back at the same table with the response from his clients: No. Too much uncertainty. They realized Murray's plan could pay off for them, but it could also backfire. Murray sighed. Sometimes he thought he knew the glass business better than the glass guys did. The incentives would work to their advantage. Why couldn't they see it? Murray wanted to hold out. The principles his predecessors wrote into the recycling program already had been diluted. He worried how other environmental advocates would view him if he gave away even more. But he looked at Edelstein and thought about his adversary's ties to Burton. He knew that Edelstein already was talking to lawmakers about scaling back Murray's bill. If glass wasn't happy, might they succeed in stopping him one more time? He did not want to come this close only to fail.

Murray realized he had no choice. He would go along with a plan that would keep the industry's break from expiring—and save the companies millions of dollars more on top of that. One of his organization's founding ideals—polluter pays—would fade even further from the law. In return, his opponents would call off their union men. And Edelstein, who once argued so eloquently against Murray's proposals, would now argue for them. Piece by piece, Murray was gaining the support of some of the Capitol's biggest players. His goal was to have the bill a done deal before it faced its first hearing in the Legislature. But he couldn't quite make it.

April 20, 1999

After a decade of frustration and months of preparation, Murray was ready to see his recycling bill move from the Capitol's back rooms to a public hearing. And for once he was confident, certain that the first vote on the measure—in the Senate Natural Resources Committee—would not be close. There were six Democrats and three Republicans on the committee. Murray needed just five senators to go his way to send the bill to the Senate floor.

But as Murray stood in the back of a packed hearing room, breathing in the stale air exhaled by his fellow lobbyists, a Senate aide, Evan Goldberg, pulled him aside. Senator Bowen, Goldberg told Murray, won't be voting for your bill tonight. Debra Bowen was a Democrat and a big fan of recycling. But Goldberg said the senator thought the state's recycling program had been corrupted. Too many loopholes, too many subsidies. She wanted it simplified. Murray frowned as he stood uncomfortably in the charcoal suit he'd changed into in his office before the hearing. Sure, he thought, the program had its defects. But Bowen knew as well as anyone that the whole thing had become an intricate political balancing act.

Simplifying the program meant taking something away from someone—probably a special interest like the grocery stores or cola makers. So even if he got Bowen's vote this night, he might lose two votes, or more, when the legislators who favored those interests learned about the new deal in the morning. If he lost Bowen now, he would need the other five Democrats on the committee to vote his way. And as he scanned the room again, he started feeling queasy. Where was Hilda Solis? She was another Democratic vote he thought was secured. Now she was MIA. He checked with her staff. They couldn't say if she would be there. Without Solis, Murray knew, he would lose his majority—and his bill. Unless a Republican were to come over to his side. But what would it take to get a Republican senator to vote for one of the biggest environmental bills of the year?

As long as Murray had been working to expand the state's recycling program, Gallo Wine, the world's largest winery, had been working to kill it. The secretive, family-owned company, founded by Ernest and Julio Gallo shortly after Prohibition was repealed, had given more than $1 million to state politicians in the past two years alone. The Gallos had used their influence to help keep most wine bottles free of deposits. But the Gallos also made their own bottles at a glass plant in Modesto. And that glass plant had a big problem. Murray knew the plant was having difficulty obeying a state requirement that 35 percent of the glass in new bottles come from recycled bottles.

Unlike the other factories, Gallo's tried to meet the recycled content standard with the least expensive used glass it could find. Contaminated with specks of paper, metal, and other trash, the glass caused all sorts of problems in the furnaces when Gallo tried to melt it down. What Gallo wanted was simple enough: a lower standard for recycled content. Instead of 35 percent of every bottle coming from recycled glass, Gallo wanted the threshold to be 25 percent—easing the burden on its furnaces. If that were in the bill, the measure would have the huge winery's support.

Murray knew the idea seemed absurd: One of California's largest bottle makers, Gallo, would get a special break, allowing it to recycle less. In return, Gallo would use its influence to help Murray get consumers across the state to recycle more. But he weighed Gallo's request against his need to build a coalition of interest groups. Opposition from the Gallos might sink the bill. He would accomplish nothing. In that light, he thought, what they were asking seemed like a small concession. So, as he was drafting the bill early in the year, he had included the provision to aid Gallo. At some point, he might need the votes they could deliver.

Senator Dick Monteith was a stout man with silver hair and a small mustache, a former egg-ranch manager who came to politics late in life. Republican and staunchly pro-business, the quiet, unassuming Stanford graduate had received a "0" rating from the California League of Conservation Voters. That meant, in Murray's view, that Monteith had the worst possible environmental record in the Legislature. He would have been the last guy in the Capitol expected to support the bill—but for one thing: Monteith came from Modesto, the home of Ernest & Julio Gallo. Gallo was the biggest private employer in Monteith's district. The company gave $15,000 to his campaign in 1998, his largest single private contribution. If Gallo, after years of opposing Murray's recycling bills, now had a reason to support one, so would Dick Monteith. And Monteith, as it happened, was one of the three Republicans on the Natural Resources Committee now seated on the dais in front of Murray.

Murray waited in the back of the hearing room as his fellow lobbyists drifted in and out, gathering in small clutches outside the door. Up front, on a riser a foot above everyone else, the senators leaned back in leather chairs listening to testimony on the bill. Senator Solis still hadn't arrived. Senator Bowen was a lost cause. Murray realized he would need Monteith's vote. Murray saw Edelstein, the lobbyist for the glass industry. For years, at moments like this, Edelstein was rounding up votes against him. Now, because of the deal they'd cut a few weeks before, they were on the same side. "What about Monteith?" Murray asked. Murray had not lobbied the senator. He knew he had no clout with a guy like that. "We've talked to him," Edelstein replied. But Murray couldn't be sure what would happen.

Finally, the committee secretary began to call the roll. Senator Tom Hayden, the committee chairman, voted for the bill, and Patrick Johnston and Dede Alpert. So did Byron Sher, the bill's legislative author. "Monteith?" the secretary called. "Aye," he responded. Murray let out his breath. Monteith had delivered—the only Republican to support the bill. His vote put it over the top. "Sometimes," Monteith said afterward with a shrug, "you have to make compromises."

Murray was making his share of compromises, too. And the bill was just out of the gate. Now, as it moved toward the full Senate, he feared his fellow lobbyists would try to pick apart the measure until it was meaningless. But lobbyists he could manage. What really worried him was the prospect of poor mothers cradling their wailing infants while they testified against his bill.

Kip Lipper was on the phone again. Murray waited for the bad news. Here it came. "You're not gonna believe this one," Lipper said. "I ran into this lobbyist in the hall. He's working for Welch's. Opposing the bill. Here's their new argument: We're taking food from babies." "What are they talking about?" Murray asked. He knew Welch's, the big fruit-juice cooperative, would do anything to kill the bill because it would raise the cost of its products by charging a deposit on its containers. But that wouldn't be the company's argument, Lipper explained.

The state food program for low-income women, infants and children—WIC—purchased fruit juice to improve nutrition among the poor. The new nickel deposit the bill proposed for big juice containers would cost WIC $1.1 million a year. That was a million bucks that wouldn't be there to spend on food and juice for the infants. Murray thought this was nuts. But he could not afford to ignore the threat, to let the argument gain traction. If he did, Welch's might find a way to arrange for a line of poor women to descend on the Capitol and testify against the bill. It was a nightmare in the making.

"We're the good guys here," Murray said. "We can't let them taint us with this." Murray and Lipper knew what they needed to do: Raid their $100 million piggy bank. The money was actually the state's, but it could be distributed through the bill they were writing. It came from the few cents that dropped into a state bank account every time someone bought a soft drink or beer and threw away the can or bottle without collecting the refund. Over the years, those pennies added up. Murray tracked the fund on his computer like it was a soaring Internet stock. It was all there in a spreadsheet, next to his marathon training schedule and the list of home-repairs he planned to undertake.

Handing out $100 million would create a special-interest feeding frenzy—which made it the perfect job for Murray. It helped satisfy his need to be loved, to be the focus of attention. His girlfriend, Heather, teased him about it. She called it his "Mark-o-centric" view of the world. Murray brushed off her ribbing. This was serious. The money could help him win votes. To get something done in the Legislature, Murray knew, you didn't always need to lobby the lawmakers. Instead, you lobbied the lobbyists. Once the powerful interest groups got what they wanted, they gave the signal to legislators and your votes came rolling in. So earlier in the spring, when opposition to the bill—now called Senate Bill 332—started mounting, Murray began working with Lipper and Senators Burton and Sher. They added provisions that would dole out the idle $100 million to private companies and public agencies with a stake in the bill.

Lipper made a good partner for Murray. Each had qualities lacking in the other. They even looked like opposites. Murray's wiry body was always in motion, his bony hands chopping the air to make one point after another. His words tumbled out in herky-jerky spasms that sometimes required him to stop, rewind the thought and start again. Lipper, stout and sturdy, spoke in a soft monotone, measuring his words to be sure to steer clear of trouble. He was a juggler and had dozens of projects in orbit at any given time. Murray—who always feared his ball would be the one Lipper dropped—was completely focused on one thing: recycling. It helped, too, that Murray was a meticulous organizer, a keeper of lists. Lipper was not. Whenever he brought Lipper a memo or a report, Murray left it on his chair so it wouldn't be buried in the mountain of paper on his desk.

Murray knew that some payments they wrote into the bill were consistent with promoting recycling. But some simply were meant to ease the bill's passage through the political pipeline. And so the frenzy began. Among the first with their hands out were the beer, glass, and soft-drink companies, which got a bigger break—now up to $40 million—on the pollution fees they paid on every glass and plastic bottle they sold. The glass and cola makers had always fought the recycling program. But friends were also in line. The trash companies that ran the curbside recycling programs were promised $15 million—tripling the subsidy they had been getting. The Local Conservation Corps, a program that employed kids to clean up the environment, wanted money and was a favorite of many lawmakers. Another $15 million out the door.

As baldly political as any payout was the $3 million that went to San Diego to expand its curbside recycling program. Why favor one city over all the others? Because a San Diego assemblyman, Howard Wayne, was chairman of the Natural Resources Committee. SB 332 would have to pass through him. Then there was the downright quirky. The director of a little outfit from Del Mar—the

Keep California Beautiful Foundation—called and said he could use some cash. Such penny-ante players were usually brushed off. But this group's honorary chairwoman happened to be Sharon Davis—the governor's wife. What was another $300,000 if it might put the bill on the governor's radar screen? Cut the check.

By late May, the handouts were working. Support was building, and the bill was sailing toward the Senate floor. Murray grew more confident. Then came Lipper's call about the threat from the Welch's guy. It was time to bring out the checkbook again. Huddling in Lipper's office, they agreed to write an amendment to the bill. One million dollars would be shaken out of the piggy bank and sent to the nutrition program to offset the new deposits on juice containers.

With days to go before a Senate vote, Murray drafted the changes and delivered them himself to the Legislature's lawyers on the third floor of the Capitol. He left a copy for Lipper. In his backpack he carried an extra—in case Lipper lost his. Sher, Lipper's boss, okayed the amendments and inserted them into the bill. And on June 2, SB 332 passed the Senate with little discussion. The vote was 25–10. The extra million had done its job. But Murray knew his work was not over. As the bill moved on to the Assembly, more opponents—and more supplicants—would be waiting. First on the agenda were the igloo people.

June 28, 1999

Murray paced nervously across the burgundy carpet of the office lobby. His stomach churned the way it did at the starting line before a marathon. His bill was in committee that afternoon, and now a nasty fight brewing between rivals in the recycling industry threatened to derail the proposal. This fight, Murray could see, had become the main event of the day, relegating the afternoon public hearing to a sideshow. The real decision was being made right now, behind closed doors, by the Legislature's two most powerful members—Senate leader Burton and Assembly Speaker Antonio Villaraigosa—and a small group of aides and lobbyists. Murray was stationed in the lobby of a nearby office suite, hoping to catch wisps of intelligence as the lobbyists and aides emerged from the negotiations and wandered past.

The underdogs in this fight were a band of traditional scrap-yard owners. They were gritty entrepreneurs in a tough business, many of them Hispanic, Korean, or Vietnamese immigrants struggling to get by in some of the lousiest neighborhoods in the state. They were outraged because their bitter rivals—the supermarket-based recycling centers—were subsidized by the state.

Murray was torn. He was an underdog himself in the Capitol and could empathize with the scrap dealers. But more than anything else he just wanted them out of the way. Any bump in the road could send his bill careening into a ditch. The scrap-yard owners, he thought, were whiners who refused to play the Capitol game. Some of them had the cash to compete in politics. What they didn't have was the nerve. As he waited, he recalled the advice he'd given the year before to Steve Young, the owner of a chain of scrap yards based in Los Angeles. Murray begged Young to plug into the political system. He even pointed him to the man he should cultivate as his champion in the Capitol: Assemblyman Howard Wayne of San Diego. He's got a tough election coming up, Murray told Young. Write him a check for five grand, then head down to San Diego and talk strategy with him a week later. Make Wayne your wedge in the system. If you want to have a prayer of winning this thing, that's what it'll take. But Young didn't do it. Now it was costing him.

The "igloo people" were just the opposite. Known for the little white, green and blue structures that dotted parking lots around the state, the supermarket-based centers were a lobbying powerhouse. The igloos looked like mom-and-pop operations. Created by the Legislature to save the supermarkets the trouble of collecting all those bottles and cans, many of them at first were run by non-profit groups or small-time entrepreneurs. But by 1999, two foreign conglomerates—one with California headquarters in Santa Ana, the other in Corona—had gobbled up most of the centers and dominated the industry. The two companies—Tomra Pacific and 20/20 Recycling—contributed to legislators' campaigns and spent big on lobbyists. And as their clout grew, so did the subsidy they got from government. At last count, the igloo people were getting $18 million a year. And it was Dick Robinson's job to help them keep that money.

Robinson, a jovial but tough-talking Vietnam veteran, represented Orange County in the Assembly for a dozen years and then set up shop as a lobbyist. His leatherneck physique became a lobbyist's paunch and jowls, and he soared to the top of his new profession. The recycling centers were paying him $10,000 a month to represent them. Murray admired Robinson. He was smart. He hustled. He knew the legislators and knew what kinds of arguments would hit home with each one. He not only represented his clients, he advised them. Part of that advice, invariably, was to contribute to campaigns. And as much as Murray hated to see money wield influence over policy, he knew it did. There was no denying it. What Robinson wanted out of Murray's bill was brash: A provision to not just keep the igloos' subsidies but increase them.

Murray knew the igloos could be an important ally in the coalition he was building. The scrap yards, on the other hand, played like the novices they were, boorishly raising hell like the small-town city council gadflies he had dealt with a decade earlier. He tried to bring them around, but that proved too much trouble. So he had cut his deal with Robinson. Murray would support raising the igloos' subsidy to $23.5 million. They'd back his bill. When the scrap dealers heard about the bargain they couldn't believe it. First they tried to kill the igloos' subsidy. When that failed, they tried to get one of their own. That idea went nowhere. So on this day they were in front of Burton and Villaraigosa in a last-minute plea for justice. If the igloos were going to keep their subsidies, they argued, at least don't let them use the money to compete unfairly with the rest of us.

Murray fretted as he waited in the office. One hour went by, then two. The scheduled time of the hearing—1:30—came and went with no resolution. The lobbyists, he heard, had shifted venues from Burton's office to Villaraigosa's. The speaker, who was already contemplating a run for mayor of Los Angeles, was being lobbied hard by a group of scrap-yard owners from his central Los Angeles district. Murray feared that if they got to him they could really muck up this deal. What if it turned into one of those pointless wars between the Senate and the Assembly? Might his bill die? But Robinson was smiling when Murray saw him enter the lobby around 2 p.m. Everything was fine, he said. He'd made just one concession to overcome the scrap dealers' concern about unfair competition: His clients would agree not to use their subsidies to pay consumers more than the scrap yards were paying for their cans and bottles. Murray was pleased. All they needed now was the blessing of the Natural Resources Committee.

Villaraigosa was already there when Murray arrived at the committee room. He watched the speaker move from member to member on the committee, whispering in each lawmaker's ear. Chairman Wayne banged his gavel. Villaraigosa found a seat in the packed room's second row. A man in the first row—the row reserved for legislators—offered up his chair. "No thanks," the boyish-looking speaker said, shaking his head and smiling. "We had our own hearing. I had a front row seat there."

This hearing, in public, was mostly for show. The dispute that had consumed most of the day was barely mentioned before the bill was okayed and sent to its next committee. Murray was happy, but still had a nagging fear: Gov. Gray Davis, notoriously slow to reveal his position on legislation, had yet to tip his hand. What, Murray wondered, was the governor thinking?

Early July, 1999

Mark Murray felt like a general who's just been handed his enemy's secret plan of attack. Having overcome most of the obstacles to the recycling bill in the Legislature, his concern had shifted to what his remaining opponents might do to influence Governor Davis. Now he knew. He stood over his office fax machine, holding a six-page memo written by a lobbyist for the Grocery Manufacturers of America. Lipper had sent it over from Senator Sher's office. Lipper didn't say how he got it, and Murray didn't ask.

The memo was explosive: The GMA, which included some of the nation's biggest grocery product companies, was plotting an $800,000 campaign to discredit Murray's bill. They were hiring extra lobbyists, buying advertising, lining up public-relations firms. The GMA also hoped to hire friends of the governor—they called them "Davis influentials"—to approach the governor on their behalf.

They wanted Davis to meet with the chief executives of some of the firms in their coalition: Kraft, Nestle, Quaker Oats, PepsiCo, Coca-Cola.

Murray fretted as he looked over the list of corporations. These were giants of American industry. They did not want their products—iced teas, coffees, sport drinks—to carry deposits on their containers. There was no way to win them over. And who knew what influence the GMA might have on the governor? Then more bad news: "They've got Vic Fazio working for them," Lipper said. That alarmed Murray. Fazio was a former Democratic congressman, a longtime Davis ally who'd helped set up the governor's Washington office. He's one of the good guys, Murray thought. And he's working against our bill.

The grocery makers also brought on Burson-Marsteller, a giant public-relations firm whose advisers included Garry South, the mastermind behind the governor's landslide victory the year before. Darius Anderson, who had run the governor's inauguration ceremonies, already was working the issue for Pepsi. Damn.

It was early July, and the Legislature was about to leave on its summer recess. "We gotta get the grass roots ginned up," Murray told Lipper. "We gotta make some noise."

Lipper told him he'd heard that one of their allies was going to leak the memo to the media. Again, Murray didn't press for details. But he thought the idea made sense. Even though everyone was lobbying the heck out of this bill, spending thousands, the GMA guys were the only ones dumb enough to put their plan on paper. Reporters would eat it up. The bill's opponents would look bad, even sleazy. The memo found its way into the hands of reporters a few days later. The stories soon followed. Their tone suggested that the GMA, by hiring people close to Davis, was doing something underhanded. Murray was thrilled. Now, if the governor opposed the bill, he'd look like he was caving to the other side's lobbying campaign.

The stories had another benefit: They energized the bill's supporters. The glass companies, the trash haulers, the recycling centers and everyone else in the painstakingly created coalition would lose if the GMA were able to stop the expansion of recycling. There wouldn't be enough money in the recycling fund to pay out all the subsidies the special interests had been promised.

A few days after the stories broke, Murray stopped by Lipper's office for an update. With the Legislature on summer break, the Capitol was half-empty. Those aides and lobbyists who remained were enjoying the respite. Wearing shorts, a T-shirt and his favorite black Nikes, Murray popped into Room 2082. Lipper said Senator Burton was confident, but he didn't want to take any chances. Burton wanted a bill that Davis couldn't possibly veto. He wanted all the interest groups behind it. What could they do to broaden support for the bill? Lipper asked.

Murray didn't want to answer. Why even bother with more amendments? They already had nearly every Democrat on their side. They could pass the bill without making changes. The governor, Murray said, wouldn't dare veto it. Let's just jam the bill through and take our chances. But Murray knew that Burton and Sher had more on their minds than this bill. Burton had other fights to pick with the governor. Sher had a bunch of bills he hoped Davis would sign. They didn't want this one to be a bigger problem than it needed to be.

The conversation turned to juice. For weeks Murray had worried that they might have to ditch the proposal to place a deposit on containers of 100 percent fruit juice. They'd already had the problem with the nutrition program. Then, at the last committee hearing, Sher had pledged to work with the fruit-juice industry to try to soften its opposition. So Murray floated a thought: They could simply exempt the big, 46-ounce juice bottles from deposits and be done with them altogether. As soon as the words left Murray's mouth, he regretted it. Was he giving in too easily? But Lipper loved the idea. There was no withdrawing it now. Murray returned to his office to draft the amendment and then went to dinner with his girlfriend, Heather. After spending most of the year fighting off enemies, he told her, now he had to worry about his friends.

The exemption for the big fruit juice containers was one more concession, one more special break for an influential interest. Murray, of course, had cut his share of deals. But those, he reasoned, were necessary to move the bill along. Now that others were doing the compromising, he no longer liked it. He thought they had taken a step backward. He hoped it would be the last. But he braced for more. Pepsi and Coke had been lurking all year, waiting for just the right moment to attack the 5-cent deposit his bill would place on 20-ounce bottles. He knew the assault on the "nickel-20" was coming. And he didn't trust his allies to fight it off.

August 1, 1999

Murray was in a foul mood. The oppressive heat of a Sacramento summer, an aching leg, and the feeling that his political allies were deserting him all had him down. He'd run three marathons and three 50-mile races since and his 36-year-old body was wearing out. He'd torn his right hamstring three times, and he was having a hard time facing the fact that his competitive running was over for a while. He hated backing off his running the way he hated backing off from a political fight.

Murray felt like he'd been giving in all year to the influential interest groups with a stake in the recycling bill. He'd caved to the wine industry, cut his deal with glass, done a favor for Gallo. He'd taken care of the trash haulers, the beer breweries, and the recyclers. He'd bent over backward to satisfy the fruit juice processors—and still they were complaining. That was enough. But as he prepared for the final public hearing on his bill to expand recycling, he worried that his strongest ally, Senator Burton, was still in a giving mood. He feared that Burton was about to deal away a very important piece of his bill: the nickel-20.

Murray's bill would double the deposit to five cents on the 20-ounce plastic bottles Coke and Pepsi started selling a few years back. Californians were gulping down 1.6 million of the super-size soft drinks every day—and few of the bottles were being recycled. A higher deposit, experience showed, would mean a higher recycling rate.

Murray also saw the proposal as the start of something bigger. If he could get the Legislature to approve a nickel deposit on 20-ounce bottles this year, in another year or two he might also double the deposit on the smaller bottles and cans. Then the program would really be complete. It would finally match the vision his predecessors in the environmental movement had sketched out a decade before. It might even be a model for the nation.

Murray knew that Ralph Simoni saw it differently. A fit, dapper man whose perpetual calm hid an intense and focused approach to the job, Simoni was the lobbyist for California's soft drink industry. He'd been fighting the nickel-20 since the day back in February when the bill was introduced. Although Simoni had other bills to lobby, the soda makers were among his biggest clients. Murray knew that killing the nickel deposit was Simoni's top priority.

Murray won all the early battles as the bill moved through two Senate committees and then passed easily in the full Senate. The proposal also survived a hearing in the Assembly Natural Resources Committee. Simoni testified at every hearing, and at every hearing the vote went Murray's way. But Murray knew that Simoni would never give up. The soft drink lobbyist organized the bottlers from all over the state. Most of them were on friendly terms with their local lawmakers, and Simoni got them to flood their representatives with letters and phone calls. Many followed up with personal visits. Their message: Murray's proposal would cost their companies and their customers $15 million a year, maybe more. The higher deposit, they said, was like a tax increase.

Murray thought this was ridiculous. The deposit was not a tax. Anyone who paid the deposit could simply return the bottle for a refund if they wanted their money back. But Republicans in the Assembly took up the antitax battle cry. Governor Davis, a Democrat trying to build a record as a centrist, listened. Finally, Senator Burton took notice. The Senate leader, working mostly behind the scenes, had shepherded Murray's bill through the Legislature to that point. His help was crucial. But for all his power and bluster, Burton had a maddening habit of giving ground to the influential companies and interest groups with a stake in the bill. He wanted things to go smoothly.

As opposition to the nickel deposit mounted, Burton started talking about ditching the proposal. He asked Lipper and another aide to negotiate with Assemblyman Keith Olberg, the leading Republican critic of the measure and a strong ally of the soft drink industry. Then, one day in mid-summer, Lipper called Murray. Olberg says he'll support the bill if the nickel-20 comes out, Lipper said. And Olberg will bring other Republicans with him. Murray argued against it. We've got the votes to pass the bill without Olberg, he said. We've already given in on fruit juice. Why give up anything else? Murray didn't know what else to say. He could not be sure what was really motivating Burton. Lipper was his best link to the Senate leader, but the aide was not always forthcoming about what Burton was thinking. The senator, Murray thought, might be playing to the Republicans and the governor. Or maybe he just wanted to score points with Pepsi and Coke.

This was frustrating. Burton wasn't debating the wisdom of the nickel deposit. He wasn't doubting whether it would lead to more recycling. Hell, just one year before, Burton had stared down the previous governor, Pete Wilson, over the exact same issue. No, this was interest-group politics at its worst, Murray thought. The policy at stake wasn't important. It was: How do we satisfy an influential lobby? The nickel-20 had been approved in public votes by the full Senate and by an Assembly committee with jurisdiction over environmental issues. Now it would be deleted from the bill without a word of public discussion—or even an explanation.

Murray felt trapped in a web of his own creation. He'd ridden with Burton and Sher to this point. His bill would never have made it this far without them. He couldn't very well abandon them now and strike off on his own, arguing in public for things they opposed. In the Capitol's unwritten rulebook, that would surely mean betrayal. He had to go along. His leg still ached. Now his head hurt, too. But he had to push on. The finish line was coming into view, but to reach it he had to get past the most volatile woman in Sacramento.

Mid-August, 1999

Carole Migden, a small, wispy New Yorker transplanted to San Francisco and the California Assembly, rattled through bills in her Appropriations Committee with the charm of a drill sergeant. Every bill that spent money had to get by her to become law. And every lobbyist dreaded the mandatory appearance. This day alone, she and her 20 colleagues would decide the fate of 300 measures. And one of them was Senate Bill 332.

Murray filed into the hearing room behind a long line of lobbyists and leaned against a wall, waiting for his turn to speak. The coat pockets of his rumpled black suit were bulging with two orange-flavored fruit drinks he'd grabbed on his way to the Capitol. He intended to whip them out to show the lawmakers how two identical bottles—one containing a carbonated drink, one not—were treated differently under the current law. One charged a two-cent deposit, the other didn't. The legislation he wrote would change that. If his bill made it by Migden's panel, Murray knew, it would pass easily in the full Assembly. More than 10 years of work would finally pay off. Today was the last real chance his opponents had to stop him.

Things moved quickly on Migden's turf. Murray listened as Senator Sher— the bill's legislative author—began to describe a set of amendments agreed to earlier, behind closed doors. Sher, a bearded, 71-year-old Harvard-educated lawyer who looked every bit the kindly professor he once was, started talking about the concessions to the fruit-juice and soft-drink companies. Migden cut him off. She peered over her glasses at Murray and the other lobbyists waiting to testify. "All those people against the wall, you're all here in support of the bill? "she snapped. They nodded. "OK. We got it. Sit down."

Murray found a spot near the front of the room and listened as Sher and a former critic of the bill, Assemblyman Olberg, took turns praising the measure. The emphasis, Murray noted, was not on what it would do for the environment, but on how it was no longer opposed by the special interests he had been court-ing. "It's a package deal," Sher said, "that has wide support." So this was how it is going to be, Murray thought. He could forget about his little juice-bottle dem-onstration.

The questions began. Assemblywoman Marilyn Brewer, a Republican from Irvine, was first. "I would like to know," she asked, "if the plastics industry was at the table and if they are in support of this bill." Sher assured her that the plas-tics industry had been taken care of. Simoni, the soft-drink lobbyist, came to microphone and confirmed that his clients had dropped their opposition.

Assemblyman Rod Wright, a Democrat who represented one of the most urbanized areas of Los Angeles, had a question. "My concern," he said, "is did the agricultural interests and the other people relative to the juices and food stuffs that get covered, did the amendment take them off of opposition?" Murray rolled his eyes. This was turning out to be a classic legislative hearing— lawmakers talking in shorthand about special-interest support for a bill while barely bothering to discuss what it would do. So he was surprised by Assem-blywoman Helen Thomson's question. "Speaking for the mothers who have to pack a lunch," she began, "tell me about the little juice bottle that has to fit into a lunch box and go with the kids to schools. Are they exempt or not?"

Here, Murray thought, was someone actually asking how the bill would work. Olberg tried to deflect it. "Some fathers do pack those lunches," he joked, eliciting laughter. "You mean the fathers that aren't drunk and hung over?" Migden asked. The audience groaned. Thomson's point was nearly lost. But Sher picked up the thread. The little juice bottles, he said, would now have de-posits on them. And they should, he said, to prompt kids to bring them home or put them in a recycling bin.

Then another question, from across the room. "The opposition," said As-semblyman Lou Papan, referring to the grocery makers, the only major interest still fighting the bill. "I wasn't clear as to why they were opposed to it, and sena-tor, why we couldn't accommodate them?" "Because," Sher said in his patient, professorial manner, "they don't want consumers who buy their products to be charged a deposit." "That is their only objection?" Papan persisted. "Yes," Sher answered. "They don't want to be under the law."

That was it. The debate, such as it was, was over. Nine minutes of discussion on one of the biggest environmental bills of the year, a measure that would add deposits and refunds to two billion cans and bottles and keep thousands of tons of trash out of the state's landfills. Migden called the roll. The bill passed with 13 votes on the 21-member committee.

Murray had been looking forward to this day for more than 10 years. But he wasn't celebrating. Winning, which he wanted more than anything else, suddenly didn't seem entirely worth it. To win, he had become part of something he believed was wrong. He'd given up independence and compromised ideals. He thought about the years he had spent trying—and failing—to get to this point on the strength of his arguments and the value of his cause. He finally won only because he had been joined by an army of lobbyists, each representing someone who stood to gain from his bill, each representing an interest group that derived its influence from the size of its checkbook.

The lawmakers who'd voted against his bills in years past did not seem to care what his proposals would do for the environment. And the ones who voted his way this year were no different. Murray had simply found a way to please the people who mattered—his fellow lobbyists—by cutting their clients in on the money that flowed through the recycling program. Then the Legislature went along.

Murray pushed that thought to the back of his mind as he pulled open the Capitol's massive wooden doors and walked out into the noon heat. For now, he was thinking about one last important chore.

Late August, 1999

Murray sat in his cluttered office three blocks from the Capitol, wondering how he could have been so stupid. In his hands he held a beautiful glass bowl he had specially ordered from a shop in Arcata, where he'd attended Humboldt State. It was a gift for Senator Burton, California's most powerful legislator. Made of recycled bottles, the amber-tinted bowl seemed the perfect token to express his gratitude to Burton at a party Murray was throwing for him in two days. Murray's bill to expand recycling was about to become law, and Burton's help was a major reason. Murray had named Burton his group's Legislator of the Year.

But as he studied the bowl, Murray realized this might be a huge blunder in the making. In the Capitol, you didn't say thank-you with tokens. You had something to say, you said it with money. Murray had walked the halls of the Capitol long enough to know that money was part of every deal. It was how you earned respect. He had seen how giving even small amounts could change his relationship with legislators.

Until recently, he'd had a tough time getting lawmakers to hear him out. Only a handful of the 120 members of the Assembly and Senate knew much about recycling, and fewer still had the patience to sift through the details. They didn't want to hear about his plan to add deposits to more cans and bottles—two billion a year—to encourage recycling. Then Murray made a few small contributions. His name suddenly appeared on the most important list in town—that of political donors. His phone began ringing. Legislators were on the other end. They offered him menudo breakfasts, golf outings, fishing trips to Catalina. But what they really offered him was their time. They wanted his money. And to get it they were willing to listen to him. That was priceless.

Murray knew the money game would never favor nonprofit groups like his. At best, he could afford to give a few thousand dollars a year to the campaigns of a handful of politicians. That was nothing amid the millions that changed hands in Sacramento every year. This was one race he could not win. But Murray also knew that in the short term, jumping into what he called the cesspool had its benefits. His job was not to reform Capitol ethics. It was to defend and expand recycling. His bill had cleared its last committee and, he was sure, would become law. But the opponents would never give up. And when it came time to put the new law into place, he knew they might try somehow to take away his gains. Even the simplest legislation wasn't lawyer-proof. A man of Burton's stature could be helpful at a time like that. He didn't want to do anything to offend him. Murray was still struggling with what to do as he returned the pretty bowl to its box, carefully laying it in its nest of white tissue paper.

A couple of days later, Murray was striding down one of the capital's shady downtown boulevards. The temperature was heading toward 94 degrees, one of those long, hot days typical of summer in Sacramento. A dry north wind shook the dust off the 100-year-old elms, magnolias, and pines outside the Capitol building. Across L Street, Murray ducked into Brannan's bar, a popular hangout where you could buy a Sierra Nevada on tap and drink it beneath a campaign poster of one of the Capitol's legendary dealmakers, Jesse Unruh. The food rolled into a back room cleared for the party. Pot stickers, mini tacos, sausage-stuffed mushrooms, artichoke fritata, roasted tomato bruschetta, fresh fruit, vegetables, and cheese—all piled high on hot trays and silver platters. Murray watched the guests trickle in: lobbyists, legislators, aides, more than 100 in all.

His girlfriend, Heather, was at his side. After dating for eight months, the two were now living together. He planned to ask her to marry him any day. She was his conscience, more easily outraged than he by the compromises he was forced to make. Murray's father and mother were there, too. Not every Sacramento lobbyist invited his parents to watch him do his job. But Murray was proud of what he did. And he was happy to share this part of his life with the people he loved.

Murray worked the room, chatting with Senator Sher, the legislative author of the bill, and Sher's top aide, Kip Lipper. Then Murray sensed it was time. He stuck one of his long runner's legs on the seat of a wooden chair, hoisted the rest of his body onto the makeshift platform and banged his fork on a cocktail glass. Murray welcomed his guests. Then he gingerly stepped down to begin his speech. His brown hair boyishly hanging over his eyes, Murray stood next to Senator Burton. The lawmaker was old enough to be his father, but he was really more the wisecracking uncle, sprinkling his conversation with enough profanity to make polite company cringe.

Reciting the short talk he'd rehearsed, Murray offered praise and thanks. "Senator Burton," he told his audience, "has been the man behind the scenes of our legislation." Burton, he said, had become a leading champion of the environment. The bill would not have had a chance without him. Then someone passed him the gift. "I have this glass bowl," Murray said, handing it to the lawmaker. "And I have—" "—A check!" Burton burst in, smiling and reaching for the $1,000 draft almost as soon as Murray pulled it from his pocket. Murray cringed—and thought: What if? What if I hadn't decided to write a check? What would Burton have thought of me then? He was at once disgusted and accepting of the game he had chosen to play. The young man who had emerged from college full of idealism about politics had become, a decade later, the ultimate insider. He had learned the Capitol's Golden Rule: Whoever has the gold, rules. Murray had been winning influence all year thanks to other people's gold. Soon he would find out what it was like to be on his own again.

February 23, 2000

Murray was getting married in three days. He should have been working with Heather Strauch on final plans for their ceremony on the beach at Point Reyes. Instead, he was in his office, trying to figure out how to convince the governor that tomatoes were a fruit, not a vegetable. If this was what winning was like, Murray thought, he might as well go back to losing.

The dispute over tomatoes was just one of many that had popped up, like dandelions in a newly planted lawn, in the 137 days since the governor signed Murray's bill into law. Murray had made a lot of unpleasant compromises to build the coalition of interest groups needed to get the bill through the Legislature. Now, after it was law, the opponents, and even some of the supporters, were still trying to mold it to their liking. Bombarding the governor's office with arguments about this word or that phrase, they pushed interpretations favoring their interests. And they were succeeding.

The glass companies had already convinced Davis that the new law allowed their pollution fees to go even lower than Murray thought he had bargained for. Kraft foods argued that the bill did not require a deposit on kids' drinks sold in the increasingly popular plastic and foil pouches. Kraft won. Now came vegetable juice.

The point of Murray's bill was to expand recycling by requiring deposits on nearly every beverage not already covered by the old recycling law. It was supposed to end confusion by eliminating most of the gaps in the law. Carbonated water, for instance, had been in, while spring water was out. Orange soda was in, orange punch was out. His bill, Murray believed, called for a deposit on any beverage not explicitly exempted.

That was how the state Department of Conservation saw it, too. The agency sent notices around the state listing the products that would carry a deposit starting January 1. The tomato juice people went nuts. A lawyer for the League of California Food Processors challenged the interpretation. The industry's lobbyists descended on the governor's office. Their view was just the opposite of the state's take on the law. Any container not listed in Murray's bill, they said, should be exempted from the two-cent deposit.

And because Murray's bill did not list vegetable drinks—it did mention fruit juice and noncarbonated soft drinks—tomato juice, they argued, ought to be out. They cited a long line of bureaucratic and legal decisions—all the way back to an 1893 U.S. Supreme Court ruling—defining tomatoes as vegetables. If they won this fight, the tomato processors would do more than exempt their juices. They'd open a loophole big enough for millions of bottles and cans to sneak through, everything from energy boosters to Kool-Aid—a product Murray hadn't been smart enough to specifically name in the bill. The measure's main goal, to end the confusing exemptions, would be subverted.

Murray tried to get Senator Sher, his longtime ally and the official author of the bill, to step in and help. Sher had written a letter to the Department of Conservation expressing his concerns. But Lipper said his boss didn't want to go any further. Murray called Senator Burton. Surely, Burton, the most powerful member of the Legislature—the man Murray's group had named its Legislator of the Year—would lean on the governor's office to counter the pressure coming from the growers and packers. But Murray couldn't get through to Burton's aide.

Murray had been in countless private meetings while he and the other players were hammering out the bill in 1999. Now, with a big part of the new law hanging in the balance, he couldn't get a seat at the table. Hell, he couldn't even find out where the table was—where and when the closed-door meetings were being held. The influential allies who had been by his side the year before—the trash haulers, the glass industry, the wineries—didn't have a stake in this fight. Without them, he was just another small-time lobbyist. He suddenly felt like the amateurs he'd seen wandering around the Capitol, clueless about the process but ever hopeful that someone might listen to them.

Murray laid a brown cardboard box on the carpeted floor of his office. Into it he placed a couple of dozen cans and bottles, examples of the kinds of containers that would be exempt if the fight over tomato juice went against him.

Ultra Slim-Fast. Drinkable yogurt. V-8 juice. Shortly before noon, dressed in blue jeans, a paisley shirt and a tattered brown sport coat, Murray hoisted the heavy box and left his building for the short but chilly walk to the Capitol. Mike Gotch, the governor's legislative secretary and a man Murray had known for years, wasn't returning his calls either. Murray hoped the box of drinks—along with a strongly written letter—would get his attention. He pulled open the door to the governor's office and looked at the secretary sitting behind a large desk in the lobby. She eyed him warily. "I have something for Mike Gotch," he said.

For security reasons, the secretary explained, you can't just drop that box and leave. Someone will have to accept it, or you'll have to take it with you. He had gone from partying with the Senate leader to being treated like the Unabomber. Gotch was out, but his secretary escorted Murray into the office and let him leave the box on the desk. Then she escorted him out again. He'd done everything he could now. It was in the governor's hands.

The beachfront wedding was marred by a steady rain that forced the ceremony indoors to a banquet room at a nearby hotel. But Murray and Heather spent a long and relaxing weekend celebrating. When he returned to the office Wednesday, news was waiting for him. A fax had come from the Department of Conservation. It was addressed to all "interested parties." Murray was interested. The state was reversing itself. Exempted from deposits, the notice said, was any beverage container not specifically included in the law. Examples: vegetable juices, Bloody Mary mix, Kool-Aid Bursts and all flavors of Slim-Fast. Millions, probably tens of millions, of containers that would have been recycled would now be thrown away.

Still on an emotional high from his wedding, Murray tried not to brood over his setback. The surviving portion of the law, he told himself, remained a major accomplishment. Nearly two billion more bottles and cans a year would find their way to recycling centers instead of landfills. But he couldn't get over the way this deal went down. It represented everything he thought was wrong with the Capitol: secret meetings, back-room negotiations, politicians bending to the will of influential contributors without bothering to seek, or accept, opinions from the public. If you had clout, you had a say. If you didn't, you were frozen out.

It was, come to think of it, pretty much the way he'd helped write the law the year before.

Appendix

Lobbyists in California are as diverse as the state itself. They represent business and labor, huge private industrial firms and small public interest groups. They work both sides of virtually every major issue from abortion and gun control to workmen's compensation and health care benefits. They devote their careers to a single client or contract out as hired guns for anyone willing to pay their fees. The four profiles included here offer a small sample of the vast range of backgrounds, experience, and training that lead people to become lobbyists

Included here as well are three charts that illustrate the financial scope and political reach of the state's major lobbying firms. They include the Top 10 Lobbying Firms, the Top 10 Employers of Lobbyists, and the amount of money spent on lobbying by industry. All the numbers are from January 1, 1999—December 31, 2000.

Art Croney

Men and women come to the arcane profession of political lobbying by many paths, but few can say, as Art Croney does, that it was a matter of divine intervention. "When I was 31 years old, in my third marriage and on the verge of making a mess of my life, I found the Lord, or he found me," says Croney, who represents the Committee on Moral Concerns.

Croney typifies dozens of Capitol lobbyists who are paid relatively small salaries, occupy inexpensive offices in older buildings (he's in the "goo-goo ghetto" at 926 J St.), have little or no ability to make or arrange for campaign contributions, and labor for causes in which they deeply believe.

The causes may be conservative ones, such as the lifestyle issues that Croney and his organization pursue, or liberal ones, such as environmentalism or gay rights. But they and their advocates are a significant subculture in the money- and power-obsessed Capitol.

Croney was working in business and doing volunteer lobbying for the California Pro-Life Council, an umbrella group that opposes abortion, when an early 1980s recession wiped out his day job. "Whenever I had spare time I was down at the Capitol," Croney recalls. "And I crossed paths with the Rev. W. B. Timberlake." Timberlake was one of the pioneer religious lobbyists and his Committee on Moral Concerns was deeply involved in the Capitol's nonstop political debates over abortion in the 1980s.

Timberlake offered Croney a job for $7 an hour and, when Timberlake retired, Croney took over the organization. He now earns about $50,000 a year—

which makes him one of the Capitol's lower-paid advocates. The committee has about 3,000 members who send in contributions.

"This is a Christian calling," says Croney. "I wouldn't do this for anyone but the Lord. I don't like politics . . . the insanity these days."

How does a conservative religious lobbying organization that's out of step with a Democratic legislative majority operate? "Every year I win a couple," Croney says, citing, among recent victories, killing legislation that would have legalized surrogate parenting and passing a measure to outlaw human cloning. But he adds, "We keep losing on these gay rights bills." With increasing Democratic majorities—including several openly gay legislators—gay rights advocates have become more vocal in pushing legislation on such matters as barring discrimination on sexual orientation or legalizing homosexual unions.

The key to winning for someone like Croney is to play on the reluctance of Democrats from conservative suburban or rural districts to do something that might alienate their conservative voters, while taking Republican support pretty much for granted. Win or lose, Croney will continue to labor as the Lord's lobbyist. "God just had me in the right place at the right time," he says.

Mike Kahl

Contract lobbyists who work for a variety of clients stand at the top the pecking order of 1,200 men and women who try to influence policy in the Capitol—and no one stands taller than Mike Kahl.

The mild-mannered former political campaign manager and staff aide heads a firm with 16 lobbyists, upwards of 70 clients (mostly corporate), and more than $4 million a year in fees. But Kahl is also something of a pioneer in reshaping lobbying techniques for the much-changed, term-limited Legislature in the 1990s—moving beyond one-on-one schmoozing to media relations, policy research, and grassroots organization.

"We try to reflect the changes in the political system," says Kahl. When term limits were enacted in 1990, he decided that a broader approach to affecting policy was needed. "The good old boy thing . . . was pretty much changed by term limits, so I reorganized this firm from straight lobbying. We try to be on top of the substance of the issue and deal with the lack of institutional memory. We do a lot of coalition-building."

Kahl came to lobbying via a well-trod path: helping politicians get elected. A political science fellowship at the University of California, Berkeley, led to a series of Republican campaign and staff jobs in California and Washington. They included a stint as chief of staff to a state senator and an aide to Bob Finch, who gave up the lieutenant governorship of California in 1969 to become Richard Nixon's health and welfare secretary. "I wanted him to run for the U.S. Senate in 1970," says Kahl, "but he decided not to run at the last minute, so I decided it was time to move on." After running his own consulting firm in Washington and California, Kahl returned to Sacramento in 1980 to start a lobbying firm. "We started as a very small operation," he says of the firm that has grown to be one of the Capitol's biggest.

The Western States Petroleum Association represents a quarter of the income for Kahl/Pownall Advocates (Kahl's partner is Fred Pownall), paying the firm nearly a million dollars a year to look after the interests of the oil industry. Other clients are a Who's Who of the contemporary California economy, including health care, energy, financial and agricultural interests, plus some nonprofit organizations such as the Community College Foundation, and such offbeat interests as the California Incontinent Product Suppliers Association.

Most Kahl clients are substantial contributors to campaigns, one of the important tools of any successful political action campaign, along with lobbying expertise and effective media/grassroots operations. Like most big firms, Kahl/Pownall employs lobbyists on both sides of the aisle, many of them former legislative or administrative staffers who are intimately familiar with the arcane ways of the Capitol. Lobbyist Rick Rollens, for example, was the chief clerk of the Senate and headed the Senate's office of bill analysis; John Geoghegan is a one-time gubernatorial cabinet member; and policy research director Loren Kaye is a former journalist.

Roxanne Miller

Government spends more to lobby the California Legislature than any other interest group. Cities, counties, and school districts are the biggest spenders thanks to the 1978 passage of Proposition 13. The ballot measure slashed local property taxes and made local governments and schools much more dependent on the state for financial support. The locals responded by beefing up what had been a relatively small corps of lobbyists—including a Capitol newcomer named Roxanne Miller.

Miller had worked briefly in the Legislature, mostly for the Senate Local Government Committee, and as a lobbyist before signing on with the city of San Jose in the mid-1970s. By the early 1980s, the ranks of local government and school lobbyists had expanded dramatically. Some, like Miller, work for individual governments; others labor at firms that do contract lobbying for large umbrella organizations, such as the League of California Cities and the California State Association of Counties, or smaller, specialized groups, such as the oddly named Association of California Cities Allied with Prisons.

The primary focus of local government and school district lobbyists is money, particularly the $50-plus billion in the state budget for aid to local government. But local government lobbyists work on other issues ranging from redevelopment reform to, in Miller's case, fees that airports charge passengers.

During the 1980s, Miller's work was made easier by having San Jose legislators chair both of the legislative budget committees. Miller could count on Assemblyman John Vasconcellos and Senator Al Alquist to protect the city in budgetary politics, though both were known for their prickly personalities.

The 1990s have been tougher for local government lobbyists. When the state ran into major budget problems early in the decade, the Legislature and Governor Pete Wilson shifted several billion dollars a year in local property taxes from local governments to schools, allowing the state to reduce its school aid. This raid on local government treasuries has been a sore point ever since, and their inability to do anything about it points up the inherent weaknesses of local government lobbyists.

Miller's most important assets are timing, her experience working with local legislators, and her ability to influence the media on issues important to her city, one of the state's fastest-growing thanks to the explosion of Silicon Valley. Miller's primary chore is getting money and assistance to cope with growing pains—support for light rail support and help with the city's ambitious downtown renewal program. A major component of the latter is a state office building named for Alquist.

Steve Thompson

Steve Thompson is a throwback, although he doesn't think of himself as an anachronism. The California Medical Association's chief lobbyist in Sacramento is a reminder of the days, barely 20 years ago, when big, multi-issue trade associations dominated the Capitol.

At one time, the CMA was the dominant voice of professional medical care in Sacramento and a virtual adjunct of the state Republican party. It called the shots on medical issues in the same way that the California Manufacturers Association—also carrying the CMA initials—and the California Chamber of Commerce personified business, the California Labor Federation spoke for organized labor and the League of California Cities and the County Supervisors Association of California reflected local government.

Those days are gone. Trade associations are now just players, albeit major ones, among many. And they often find themselves fighting other interest groups from the same fields—as in the CMA's wars with medical specialties over "scope of practice."

The power of big associations began to wane in the late 1970s when rivals arose to press narrower causes. Smaller groups found that they could defeat seemingly more powerful umbrella organizations by making it clear that their interests were few. Legislators realized they could vote against a big organization on one issue and make it up on another bill. That led multi-issue groups to set up single-issue subsidiaries. Business organizations, for example, created a special lobby to focus on worker's compensation after suffering a multibillion-dollar defeat in 1982.

Thompson came to the CMA in 1992 after a long stint on the legislative staff, including a hitch as former Speaker Willie Brown's chief of staff. Thompson was a health care specialist in several of his staff jobs, and, as head of the Assembly Office of Research, led a drive to create a comprehensive health care access program for California.

"This is the longest I've been in any job," he says of his nine-year CMA career. Although Thompson and his staff deal with dozens of bills during a legislative session, he says working for a trade association, rather than a contract lobby firm, means that "a single set of values" governs policy.

"The techniques are pretty much the same," he says. "You get to know your subject and the legislators, and it helps to have political clout behind you." The latter refers to CMA's large political action committee, which funnels money to friendly legislators and candidates.

One major change in CMA's approach to the Legislature in recent years has been bipartisanship—one denoted by Thompson's own background as a Democratic staffer. All of the big trade groups play both sides of the aisle these days, much to the chagrin of their formerly exclusive political partners.

Top 10 Lobbying Firms
January 1, 1999 – December 31, 2000

	Cumulative Payments Received
Kahl/Pownall Advocates	$8,514,368
Robinson & Associates, Inc., Richard	$5,586,689
Nielsen, Merksamer, Parrinello, Mueller & Naylor LLP	$4,932,744
Governmental Advocates, Inc.	$4,730,786
Carpenter Snodgrass & Associates	$4,645,987
Rose & Kindel	$4,390,310
Read & Associates, Aaron	$4,299,928
Platinum Advisors, LLC	$4,064,632
Livingston & Mattesich Law Corporation	$3,871,600
Heim, Noack, Kelly & Spahnn	$3,816,986

Source: Secretary of State's office.

Top 10 Employers of Lobbyists
January 1, 1999 – December 31, 2000

	Cumulative Expenditures
California Teachers Association	$5,742,924
Pacific Telesis Group and its subsidiaries	$5,160,857
Western States Petroleum Association	$3,862,287
California Chamber of Commerce	$3,580,571
Edison International and subsidiaries	$3,110,820
California Healthcare Association and affiliated entities	$2,699,098
California Medical Association, Inc.	$2,697,448
California Manufacturers Association	$2,435,296
State Farm Insurance Companies	$2,383,542
Consumer Attorneys of California	$2,318,112

Source: Secretary of State's office.

Lobbying Expenditures By Industry
January 1, 1999 – December 31, 2000

	Cumulative Expenditures
Government	$52,863,146
Health	$41,488,510
Miscellaneous	$39,360,377
Manufacturing/Industrial	$34,571,748
Finance & Insurance	$29,664,686
Education	$27,454,973
Professional/Trade	$20,571,294
Utilities	$19,719,214
Oil & Gas	$13,621,906
Labor Unions	$12,733,617
Real Estate	$10,153,880
Entertainment & Recreation	$8,579,489
Agriculture	$7,294,794
Transportation	$6,498,619
Legal	$6,438,073
Public Employees	$5,526,256
Merchandise/Retail	$5,225,239
Lodging/Restaurants	$2,010,068
Political Organizations	$542,761
TOTAL	**$344,318,650**

Source: Secretary of State's office.

Glossary

The Capitol, like any site of highly specialized work, has developed its own jargon, one that outsiders may find puzzling if they attend legislative hearings but one that any true insider must know to communicate and function effectively. Here are some of the terms that one might hear in the Capitol's hallways:

Engine driving the train—When a lobbyist has a bill that could be unpopular, one way to aid passage is to connect it with something that is popular. The popular provision thus becomes the engine but the lobbyist is more concerned with what's in the train.

Floor jockey—The legislative author of a bill carries it on the floor of his own house, but when the measure reaches the other house, one of its members will be designated as a "floor jockey" to present it to the house, answer questions, and in all other respects act in the place of the author.

Goo-goos—It's shorthand for "good government types," meaning lobbyists for public interest and/or nonprofit groups with ideological or philosophical agendas, such as political reform, protecting the environment, or enhancing prisoners' rights. The "goo-goo ghetto" is an older office building at 10th and J streets whose proximity to the Capitol and cheap rents make it popular with such groups.

Gutted—What happens to a bill when its contents are stripped out and a new measure is inserted. See "low-ball" below.

Horseshoe—It's the Capitol's name for the suite of offices occupied by the governor and his senior aides in the Capitol's southeastern corner. It's more or less analogous to the White House's west wing, while the "Corner Office" refers specifically to the governor, just as the Oval Office symbolizes the president.

Important—Presumably, all bills are important to someone, or they wouldn't be carried. But when a lobbyist tells a legislator that a particular bill is "important," it implies that the group's decisions on campaign contributions will hinge on the politician's vote.

Juice—In brief, it means money, particularly campaign contributions. Thus, a "juice bill" is one involving moneyed interests on one or both sides and therefore likely to generate campaign contributions, and a "juice committee" is one that handles many special interest matters, such as gambling, managed health care or professional licensing and regulation. Sometimes it's called "grease," which inspired one reporter to comment about a bill on the Assembly floor: "There's enough grease here to fry a dinosaur."

Low-ball—A verb meaning to slip a bill through the Legislature so quickly or sneakily that the opposition cannot react to kill it. Certain legislators or certain lobbyists may become known as "low-ball artists" for their facility, often in the last, frantic days of a legislative session. The techniques of effective lowballing have evolved with changing legislative rules with the "floor amendment" being the current favorite. A bill pending on one floor of the Legislature is gutted, an entirely new bill is inserted as an amendment, and the measure is rushed through two floor votes and onto the governor's desk before any opposition can develop and react, sometimes in just a few hours.

Mom-and-pop—A phrase often uttered in legislative hearings to describe the impact of a bill, roughly meaning that its effects are felt largely by small businesses, or that small firms are exempted, as in "This doesn't hurt the mom-and-pops." Helping small businesses, or exempting them from the impact of an expensive regulatory or benefit scheme, is often a goal of lobbyists because, it's assumed, small business owners can be an effective bloc if their interests are involved. But the definition of a "mom-and-pop" is very elastic and completely situational.

Off the bill—An interest group may be opposing a bill but moves to neutrality when it is changed to take care of the group's concerns. The group is then said to be "off the bill."

On call—After an initial roll call vote on a bill, either in committee or on the floor, proponents or opponents can suspend voting by placing the measure "on call" while additional votes are garnered, or legislators can be lobbied to change their votes.

Renting—A word that describes a legislator who has agreed to vote in a way that may violate his principles, as in "He has not sold his vote but is renting it."

Scorecard—Various interest groups maintain records on how legislators vote on matters that affect them and produce scorecards, some for external publication and some for internal use, which indicate how well the lawmakers adhere with the groups' positions. Legislators often use these ratings in their campaign materials.

Soft kill—A bill is rejected outright when it comes to a vote in committee or on the floor of a legislative house and fails to acquire enough votes for passage. But a soft kill is having a bill held in committee without a vote, perhaps with a coating of sugar such as being referred to "interim study," a euphemism that allows the author of the bill and/or lobbyists to tell proponents that the measure is still alive when, in fact, it's been suffocated. A soft kill on the floor may result from taking a private test vote inside the majority party caucus. Having lost behind closed doors, the author of the bill knows better than to try a public floor vote.

Speakerize—Another verb that refers to the speaker of the Assembly having declared his interest in seeing a particular bill passed or defeated. It became a very important factor during the 30-year era of the strong speaker, topped by the 14-plus-year reign of the self-proclaimed "Ayatollah of the Legislature," Willie Brown. Even rumors that a bill had been "speakerized" could affect its fate and, of course, lobbyists schemed constantly to have the speaker take their side. When the speakership weakened due to term limits, it became a much less important factor, but didn't disappear altogether.

Take a walk—Under the California Legislature's rules, unlike those of Congress, it takes an absolute majority of a committee's membership or the full house to pass any bill (two-thirds on the floors for some measures). Thus, the refusal to vote on a bill has exactly the same effect as a "no" vote. When a legislator absents himself from a committee or floor session to avoid voting on a bill, he is said to have "taken a walk." And lobbyists on the negative side of an issue often encourage it.

Third House—The universal term for the 1,200-plus lobbyists who work the Capitol, implying its equal stature with the two official houses of the Legislature. The origins of the term are unclear, but it's been used for as long as anyone alive and working in the Capitol can remember.

28.8—It means a section of the legislative rules, but it's used as a verb. To 28.8 a bill means to get it moved out of the appropriations committee of a house without a hearing. Technically, it's supposed to be applied only to bills that have no fiscal impact, but the designation is a purely arbitrarily one. To advocates of a bill, it's a way to bypass one hurdle and to opponents, it's something to be avoided because it denies them an opportunity to block the measure. It's usually invoked only in the Senate Appropriations Committee at the discretion of the chair. In the Assembly Appropriations Committee, the chair often determines in advance—and in private—which bills will be passed and which will be held and then announces the decree as each bill comes up.

Walk-in-the-park—When lobbyists and legislators want to engage in an absolutely private conversation, without any chance of being overheard, they will walk in Capitol Park, which surrounds the Capitol. But the illusion of privacy was shattered when it was revealed that Alan Robbins, a state senator snared in a federal corruption investigation, took a walk in the park with insurance lobbyist Clay Jackson, but wore a secret surveillance microphone. The recording of their conversation, dealing with a payoff to Robbins to get a certain bill passed, put Jackson in federal prison and but bought Robbins a much-reduced sentence.

WORF—It's an acronym that's become a verb. "WORF" means "without reference to file," itself a jargon phrase referring to the increasingly common practice of bills being taken up on legislative floors, particularly in the Assembly, outside of the usual order on the agenda, or "file," of business. WORFING a bill means that it is being fast-tracked, usually at the behest of legislative leaders, to give opponents little opportunity to react. See "low ball" above.

Work the floor—When an initial roll call vote on a bill fails to produce the required majority or two-thirds vote, the measure is routinely placed "on call." The author of the measure, or the "floor jockey," will confer with lobbyists pushing the measure and then "work the floor," trying to round up enough votes to gain passage on a subsequent roll call. Opponents, of course, will do the same. Those working both sides will walk around with tally sheets in their hands, trying to persuade individual members to vote one way or the other.

INDEX

Zanelli, Jerry, 31

Zelman, Walter, 54

The Authors

As a young lobbyist for the League of California Cities Jay Michael devised a legislative strategy that allowed cities to tax hotel rooms, providing a generous revenue stream for hundreds of cities. He engineered the formation of the Southern California Association of Governments and led the lobbying effort to create the Los Angeles Metropolitan Transit Authority. As vice president of the University of California during the student revolts of the 1960s and '70s, he convinced the legislature to defeat constitutional amendments that would have destroyed UC's autonomy and to maintain a high level of financial support during that tumultuous era. Michael left UC in 1976 and represented physicians and health care interests for 24 years. He retired in 2000 after more than 40 years as one of Sacramento's leading lobbyists.

Dan Walters has been a journalist for more than 40 years. He joined *The Sacramento Union*'s Capitol bureau in 1975, just as Jerry Brown began his governorship, and became the *Union*'s Capitol bureau chief. In 1981, Walters began writing the state's only daily newspaper column devoted to California political, economic, and social events and in 1984, he moved to the *Sacramento Bee*. His column now appears in more than 50 California newspapers. He is the author of *The New California: Facing the 21st Century,* a widely used college text about socio-economic and political trends in the state, the founding editor of the *California Political Almanac,* and a frequent guest on national television news and public affairs programs commenting on California politics.

Daniel Weintraub has covered California government and politics for 15 years. He was a Capitol correspondent with the *Los Angeles Times* for eight years and Capitol Bureau Chief for the *Orange County Register* for six years. In November 2000, he was named California columnist for the editorial pages of the *Sacramento Bee*.